AN ABC OF LACE PATTERNS

by

GILIAN DYE

THE ELVISTON PRESS
BOSTON SPA
ENGLAND

An ABC of Lace Patterns
by Gilian Dye

First published in the United Kingdom
by The Elviston Press 1994

© Gilian Dye 1994

All rights reserved. No part of this publication may be reproduced, stored in a retrieval system, or transmitted, in any form or by any means, electronic, mechanical, photocopying, recording or otherwise, without the prior written permission of the Publisher.

British Library Cataloguing-in-Publication Data
A catalogue record for this book is available from the British Library.

ISBN 0 9522709 1 9

Printed by The KOJ Group
for The Elviston Press, 40 Heath Drive, Boston Spa,
West Yorkshire, LS23 6PB

AN ABC OF LACE PATTERNS

CONTENTS

			Page No.
Introduction			4
Abbreviations and definitions			5
Equipment and materials			5
A	for	Alphabet	6
B	for	Bookmark	8
C	for	Candle	10
D	for	Dinosaur	12
E	for	Elephant	14
F	for	Flower	16
G	for	Goldfish	18
H	for	Horseshoe	20
I	for	Icicle	22
J	for	Juggernaut	24
K	for	Key	26
L	for	Lavender bag	28
M	for	Mat	30
N	for	Necklace	34
O	for	Octopus	36
P	for	Penguin	38
Q	for	Queries	40
R	for	Rabbit	46
S	for	Seahorse	48
T	for	Teddy Bear	50
U	for	Unicorn	52
V	for	Valentine	54
W	for	Wheel	56
X	for	Cross	58
Y	for	Yacht	60
Z	for	Zebra	62

INTRODUCTION

This is a book of patterns prepared with children in mind, but suitable for anyone who has mastered the basic techniques of bobbin lace.

Basic stitches are described briefly on the next page, further hints are given in 'Q for Queries'. Specific techniques are included with patterns as they are needed.

If you are relatively new to lacemaking, work the Bookmark first, then the Candle before going on to one of the simple braid patterns such as the Valentine outline.

Any pattern requiring many 'sewings' (see over) or the insertion of beads will be easier if you have first worked the Icicle. If you are new to torchon ground, work the Goldfish before trying a more difficult pattern such as the Elephant.

To prepare the patterns: photocopy, or carefully trace (in ink not pencil), taking particular care with position of the dots as these represent pin holes. Then either cover with a stiff tracing film, or pin pattern over thin card. All the patterns requiring 'sewings' are worked with the right side on the pillow so when they are turned over any knots will be on the back.

Specific instructions have been given for working each example, but these are only starting points. Be prepared to experiment and develop your own individual pieces. Patterns can be enlarged or reduced (using a photocopier) – remember to choose a suitable thread for the new size – different combinations of stitches or colours used, or beads introduced. . . . .

DEFINITIONS AND ABBREVIATIONS

cross (cr) | X | twist (tw) X X

whole stitch (wst) – cr.tw.cr.

half stitch (½st) – cr.tw.

double (dbl) (dbls) – cr.tw.cr.tw.

(In these diagrams 1 line = 1 thread)

pair (pr) (prs) – 2 threads or 2 bobbins
Workers (wks) – the pr that goes from side to side in a braid.
Passives – the prs that travel along the braid.
Left (L): lefthand (LH)
Right (R): righthand (RH)
Plait – 2 prs worked in a series of tw.cr.

Diagrams like this show a pair as a single line;
where two lines cross a wst should be worked;
where there is a dash the pair is twisted,
– 2 twists if two dashes, etc,
(see W for Wheel).

EQUIPMENT AND MATERIALS

You will need standard bobbin lace equipment: pillow; cover cloths; pins; pincushion; bobbins; fine crochet hook (0.60).

The following threads have been used for most of the samples in the book: Coton Perle no. 8, Special Dentelles (80) or Sylko sewing cotton. These threads come in a variety of colours and are readily obtainable from craft shops or haberdashery departments. Other threads of similar thickness could be used, such as Tanne 30 or Machine Broder 30 in place of Sylko. Small beads are needed for a number of the designs.

for alphabet

The simplest way of producing any letter in lace is to work it in the Honiton lace braid known as 'rib' or '10-stick'. This is a quickly worked braid, using 5 pairs with pins on one side only – the outside of a curve.

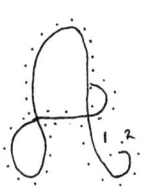
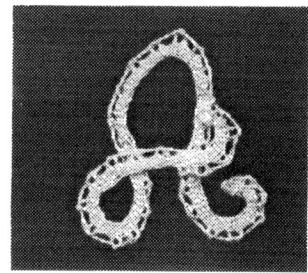

For the A start with 5prs Sylko hung across pin 1.

Twist pr on R twice.
*Take 3rd and 4th bobbins from L to work
[2 wst. tw wks x2. wst. tw both prs x2]
pin beside the stitch.
2nd row: take 2nd pr from R to work
[3 wst then an extra tw.cr with LH pr]
Repeat from * until the point where pins are on LH side, then reverse L and R in instructions, beginning with either row.

Starting the ten-stick braid

2nd row of braid

Where the braid crosses itself make a <u>sewing</u> as follows:
Remove the pin;
put a crochet hook through the loop;
tw wks from the braid;
pick up lower thread with hook,
and pull through loop;
thread other wk bobbin through new loop;
pull tight, tw;
continue with braid.
Make sewings in this way wherever two braids touch or cross, or threads finish.

Working a 'sewing'

Finish by turning back 1pr then sewing other pairs to edge of braid and working a Bruges tie (see Q.3c).

The other letters, given as section headings, are worked in a similar way — started at a free end and sewn off to the braid already worked. Most are a continuous braid, but in some a second braid is needed, this should also be started at the free end and sewn off to finish.

NB all the section heading letters are shown the right way round, so for working should be traced and the tracing turned over — this allows knots to be at the back of the work.

B for bookmark

This pattern gives practice in the basic stitches – whole stitch (wst), half stitch (½st), doubles (dbl) – and shows some of the ways in which they can be grouped for simple braids.

Wind 9 pairs with No. 8 Coton Perle.

Start with 2prs (passives) hung across each of a,b,c and d, and 1pr (workers) on e.
Work to the right with:
[8 wst. tw wks twice. pin at 1.]
Continue working section A in wst with 2tw at pins until workers reach pin x. Twist every pair once and work a row of dbls from x to y.

For section B work: [dbl. 6 ½st. dbl. pin.] on every row.

Work a row of doubles across x - y (and at each of the later narrow points).
Note: when going from dbls or ½st the pairs are already twisted, but when going from wst to dbls (or ½st) pairs need to be given a twist.

For section C work: [4 wst. tw wks x2. 4 wst. tw wks x2. pin] on every row.

Section D: *leave outside pair and take other pair from dbl to work [6 ½st. dbl. pin beside the stitch (see diagram)], repeat from*.

Section E: [3 wst. tw wks. 2 wst. tw wks. 3 wst. tw wks. pin] on each row.

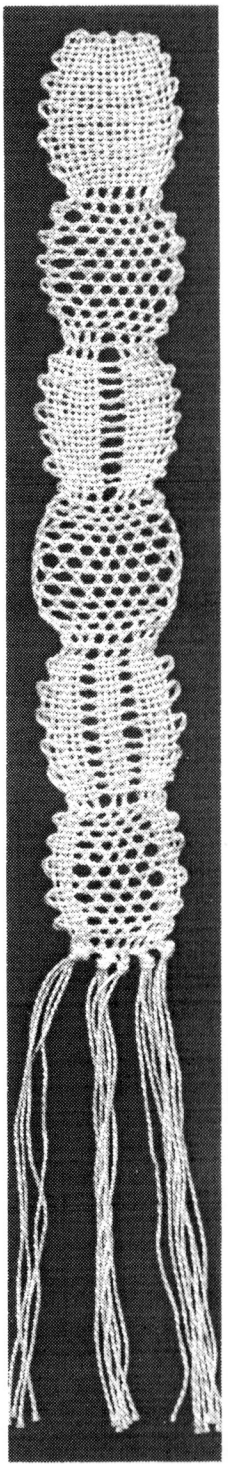

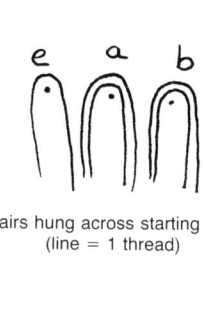

Pairs hung across starting pins
(line = 1 thread)

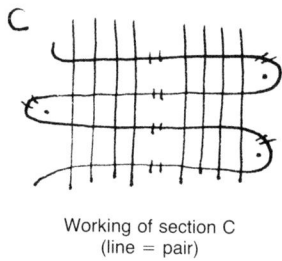

Working of section C
(line = pair)

Edge of section D
(line = thread)

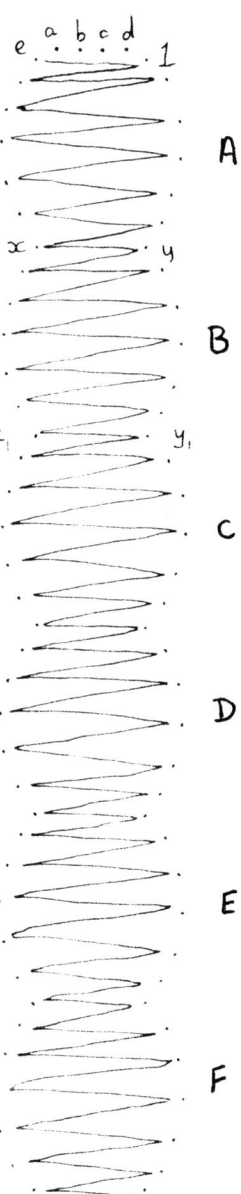

Section F: [2 wst. tw wks. 4 ½st. 2 wst. tw wks. pin]

Finish with a row of dbls, then cut threads approx 8cm from work and tie together two or four threads with an overhand knot (see Q.3a). Trim across ends of thread to neaten. Remove pins carefully.

 **for candle**

Worked with Coton Perle 8.

Flame
Hang 4prs across A
Starting on the left work
[dbl. ½st. dbl. pin at 1]
[dbl. ½st. dbl. pin at 2].

Hang a new pr on 2, placing bobbins as 3rd pr from outside.

The next 2 rows will be:
[dbl. 2 ½st. dbl. pin]
Add a pair on 4 — next row:
[dbl. 3 ½st. dbl. pin] then one on every row until 10 prs are in use.

Continue in ½st with dbls on each edge until flame begins to narrow (x).

Discard a pr at each pin until 4 prs remain.
To discard a pair: work to within 2 prs of pin, put these prs together to act as one pr for working the dbls before and after the pin, then turn back one of each of the double threads (threads can be trimmed close once the pins are removed).

Candle
Keeping the 4 pairs from the flame as passives hang on 10 more prs passives (on arrowed pin holes) and 1pr wks plus 1pr passives on B.

Starting on the left work
[15 wst. pin at C].

The candle can then be worked entirely in wst, or, as here, a pattern of holes made by twisting passives and/or workers.

When the work reaches D finish with a Bruges tie (see Q.3c) and cut close.

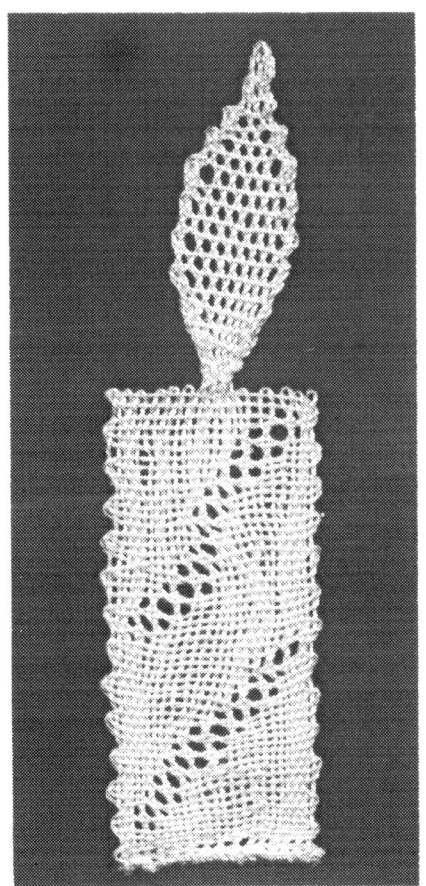
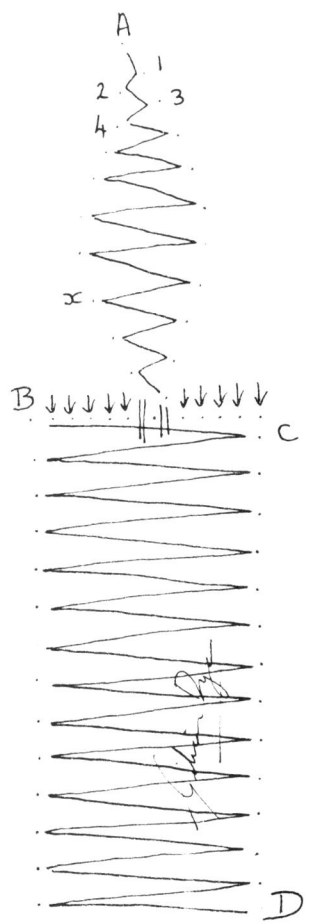

# D for dinosaur

9 prs Special Dentelles.

Start with 2prs across A, 1pr on each of B & C. Take LH on A as wks to work head in wst (tw wks at pins) adding a pair at each of the pins 1-5 – hang pr on pin placing bobbins as 2nd and 4th passives from edge.

For the eye tw wks between the two middle passive pairs then tw these passives.
On the next row tw wks only.

Discard 1pr from centre of passives at D and change the braid to: [dbl.5wst.tw wks.dbl.].
Also discard prs at E and F (reducing to 3 the number of wst worked on each row).

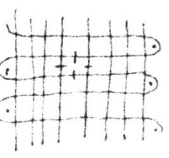 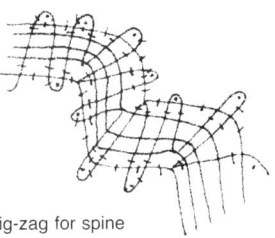

Working eye   Zig-zag for spine

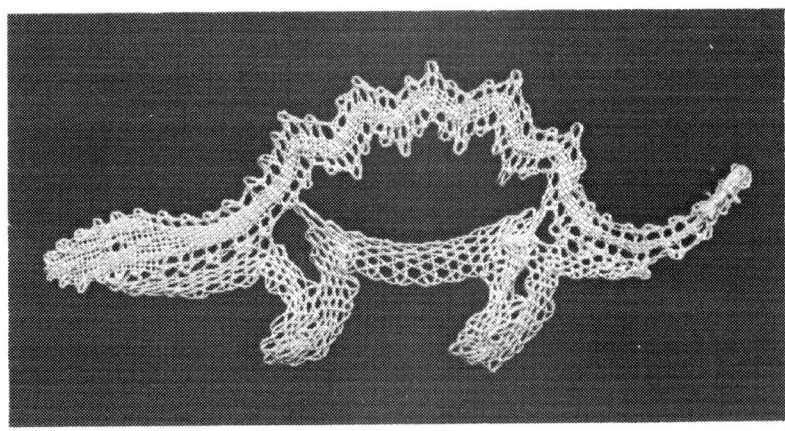

For the zig-zag spine: work 3rd wst, take these passives as wks for next 2 rows, work inside dbl (no pin) and take the edge pair as new wks.
These turns are worked alternately to L and R.

Discard 2prs towards tip of tail, plait the remaining pairs, turn back and tie down with discarded pairs.

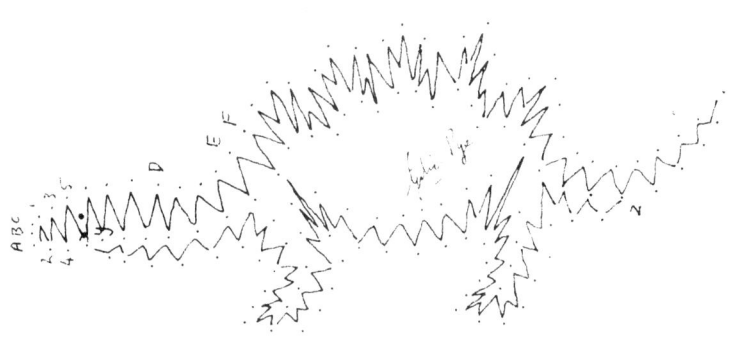

For the underbody sew in 2prs at x, 1pr at y, work in ½st adding a pair on each of the next two rows and making sewings to edge of head and neck.
For the sharp angles on the legs pins need to be used more than once and turning stitches worked, ie an inside pair is worked and the passive taken as wks for the next rows.

After each sewing on the underside of the tail work a dbl and discard the passives (tie these threads with a reef knot before cutting off).
Sew off final 2prs at z.

 *for elephant*

19 pairs Coton Perle 8.
Start at the front foot with 2prs hung on each
of pins A-D, linking the threads as in diagram.

Work a triangular tally (see Q.4c) for the first toe using 1pr from B and 1pr from C, work second toe with other pair from C and a pair from D.

Work leg in ½st. pin. ½st ground – see G for Goldfish – (for firmness put an extra twist on edge pair).
Stop at the line of pins before the solid line adding a new pair at E (hung on support pin S).

Next work trunk in ½st. pin ½st, starting with 2 prs linked at F and adding a pair at each of the pins marked ▼ (use support pins U and P).
Work in the direction shown by arrows. Where there is a double arrow follow the ½st after the pin with another ½st. pin. ½st.
Add a pair on G and complete working up to solid line.

Turn the pillow and work from top of head along back adding 3 more pairs where indicated.
Work a tally for the eye (or insert a small bead – see I for Icicle).

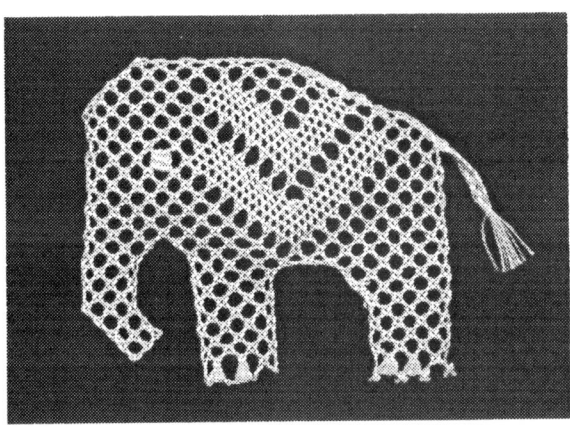

The back can be worked entirely in ½st. pin. ½st, or other torchon features may be included. In the sample two half stitch trails have been used, these are marked on pricking.

From H start discarding pairs as follows: *work a dbl with 2prs after the pin, treat each of these prs as a single bobbin to work ½st. pin. ½st at next edge pin, turn back 1 bobbin from each of the double pairs.
Repeat from * until 5 prs have been turned back.
Keep remaining extra pairs in use along back line, treating 2 or more threads as 1 as required.
Turn pillow at next solid line.

Leave 4prs at I – plait these to form the tail.
Work down rear leg discarding a pair at each x.
Finish with tallies for toes and ½st. pin. ½st at final pins.
If the motif is to be mounted on fabric these threads can be taken through the fabric, otherwise tie off at each pin with a small Bruges tie (see Q.3c). Trim discarded threads close to work once pins have been removed.

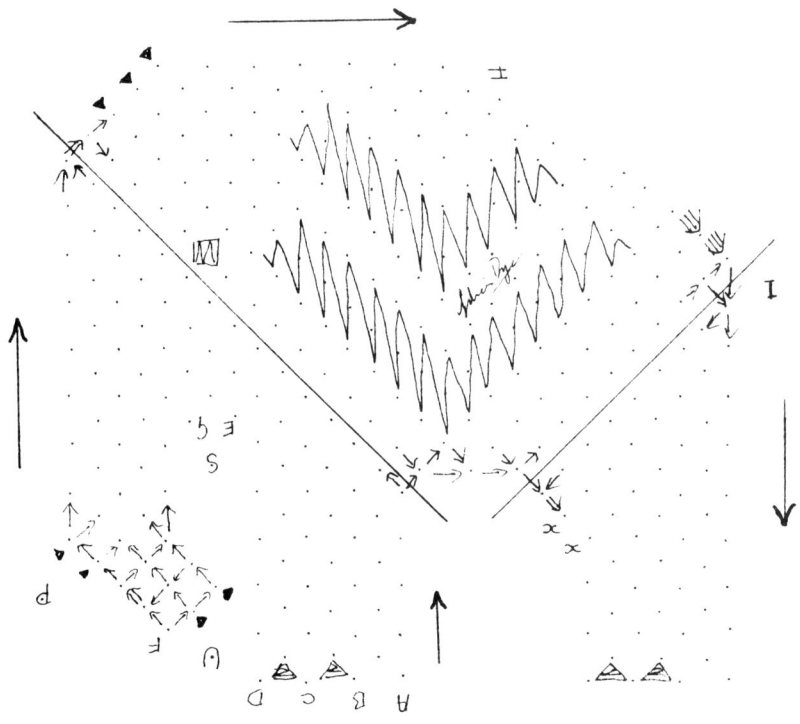

F for flower

This is worked flat, then gathered to give a 3-D flower which can be used in many ways.
Use a thread such as Special Dentelles for the larger size, Sylko or finer for the smaller.
Work with 7prs hung on as indicated.
A contrast can be used for the single pair which is only worked at pins P and should not be twisted at all.
Starting on L work:
[5 dbls. wst. pin at P.tw wks.wst.tw wks].
* 2nd row: [4 ½st.dbl.pin].
   3rd row: [dbl.4 ½st.pin].
Repeat 2nd and 3rd rows until next pin P is reached when the straight pair should be included with:
[wst.tw wks.pin.wst.tw wks].
Repeat from * to end.
After the last pin P work a row of dbls and tie off with a Bruges tie (see Q.3c) NOT including the straight thread. Remove from pillow, pull straight pair gently to gather.

The gathering thread can then be used to sew bought stamens, or a bead or a small group of leaf-shaped tallies (see Q.4a) in the centre.

The flower may be backed by fabric or paper leaves or ones made of lace — a pattern is given for a leaf which could be worked in the same way as the Candle flame, but keeping all the threads in until the end — 10prs used for the sample.

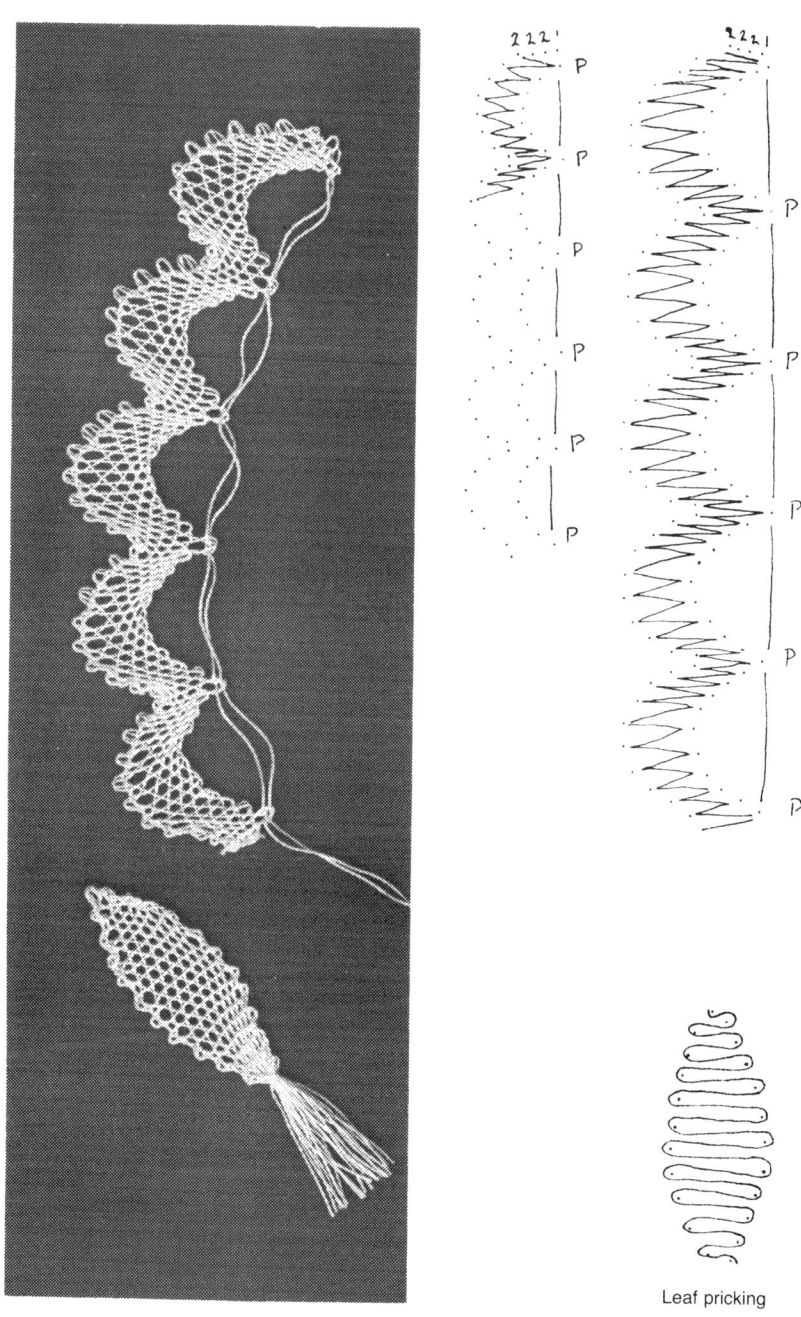

Leaf pricking

# for goldfish

16 pairs Coton Perle 8.

Hang a pair on each of the support pins A and B.
Work [½st. pin at 1. ½st].
Remove threads from support pins and pull tight around pin 1.

* Hang another pr on A, work
[½st. pin at 2. ½st] with LH pr from 1, remove loop from A and pull down.

Repeat from * bringing in new prs to work
[½st. pin. ½st] at each of pins 3-8.

Pairs hung on support pins for start   First 2 pins worked

Work pins 9-15 in the same way, using the RH pr from 1 and new prs hung on support pin B.
Now work the body of the fish in torchon ground,
ie [½st. pin. ½st] starting with prs from 2 and 9 to work pin 16.

Make the eye at ■ either by working a square tally
(see Q.4b) or inserting a bead (see I for Icicle).
When pairs reach the edge of the work (x) they can be cut and tied in an overhand knot (see Q.3a).
Rewind pairs to add at arrowed pin-holes for working the tail.
Tie off 2prs at a time at end of tail.

Arrange the loose ends and trim to give fins of an appropriate length.

This is a basic form which could be extended, or varied by using a combination of colours and/or different torchon stitches.

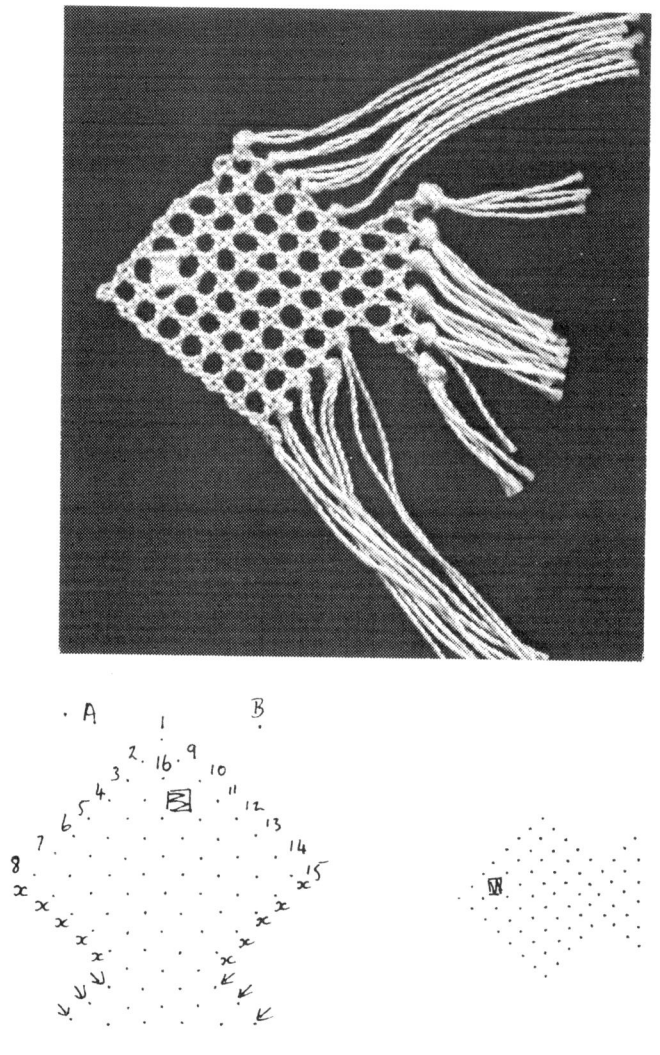

The small scale version of the pattern is suitable for working as earrings using Sylko or a fine metallic thread.

H for horseshoe

Start of horseshoe

10 pairs Sylko.

Start with 2prs on each of A-E
Work 4 rows wst.
Tw every pair x2
Work 4 rows wst.
Next row: [5wst.pin.wst], take one of these prs to L and one to R as wks for a small wst triangle (see L for Lavender bag). Continue horseshoe with triangles on L, torchon ground (see G for Goldfish), [dbl.pin.dbl] on R, and central spiders. Finish to match start with rows of wst. and twists. Bruges tie (see Q.3c). Fold each end along the twisted row and stitch down.

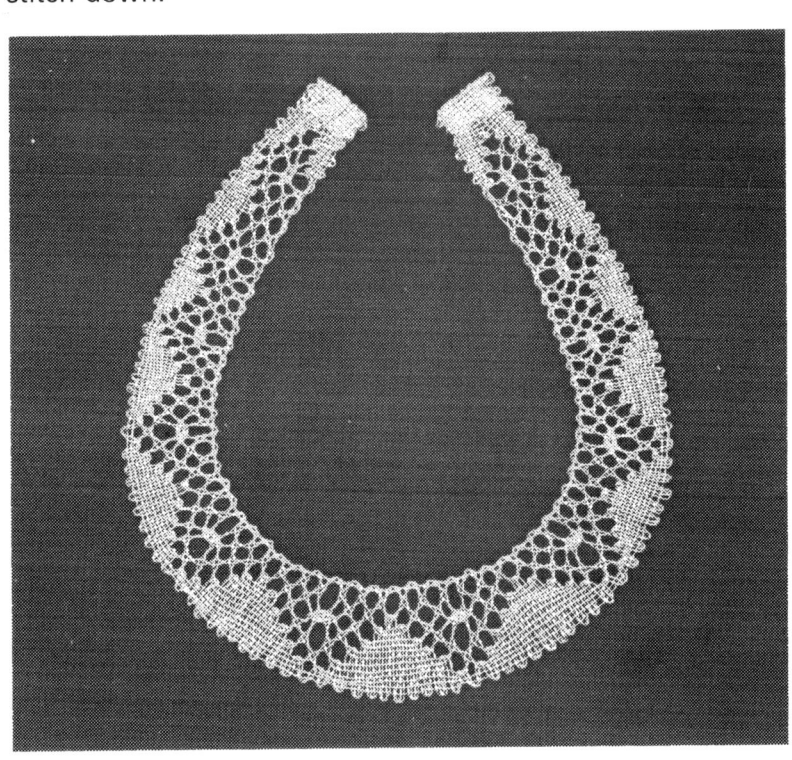

For the spiders tw each of the 'legs' (W-Z) x3,
* wst pr X through Y and Z
   wst pr W through Y and Z. * Pin in centre.
Repeat from * to *.
Tw legs x3.

Working a spider

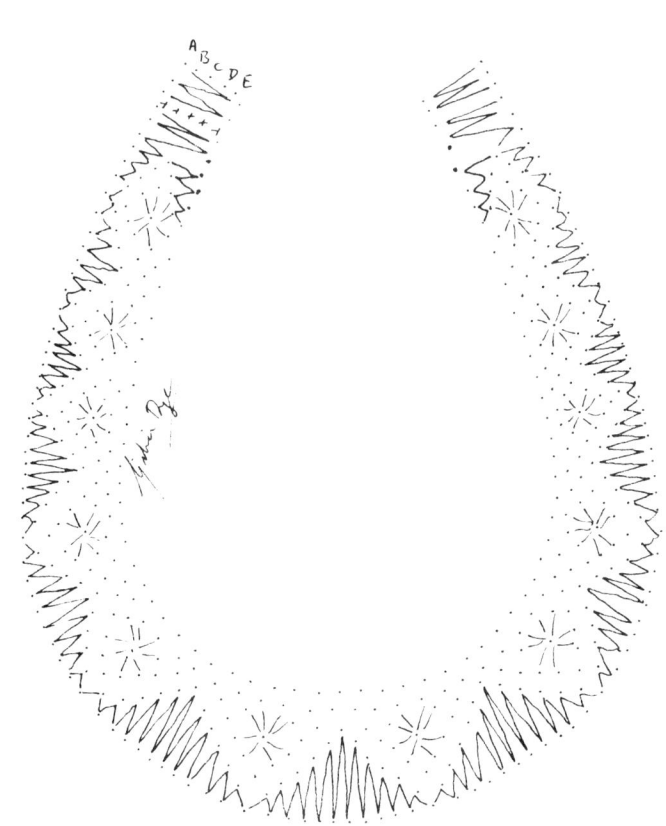

 *for icicle*

4prs Coton Perle 8 + 13 small beads.
A fine crochet hook (0.60) will be needed.

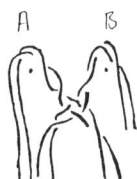 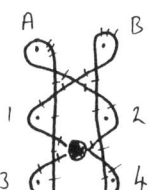

Start with 2 prs across each of A & B. Twist 3 times.
Work a dbl at each pin then:
* dbl with 2 centre pairs,
[dbl.pin at 1. dbl], [dbl. pin at 2. dbl].
Now insert a bead between the two centre pairs as follows:
slip a bead on to the crochet hook;
with the hook catch one of the centre threads and pull it through the bead;
pass a bobbin from the other side through loop;
pull bobbins apart to ease bead into position;
twist pairs on each side of bead.

Work [dbl. pin at 3. dbl] with 2prs on L,
then   [dbl. pin at 4. dbl] on R.

Repeat from *.

After pins x & y cut threads approx 8cm from work;
tie each group of 4 threads in an overhand knot
(see Q.3a).

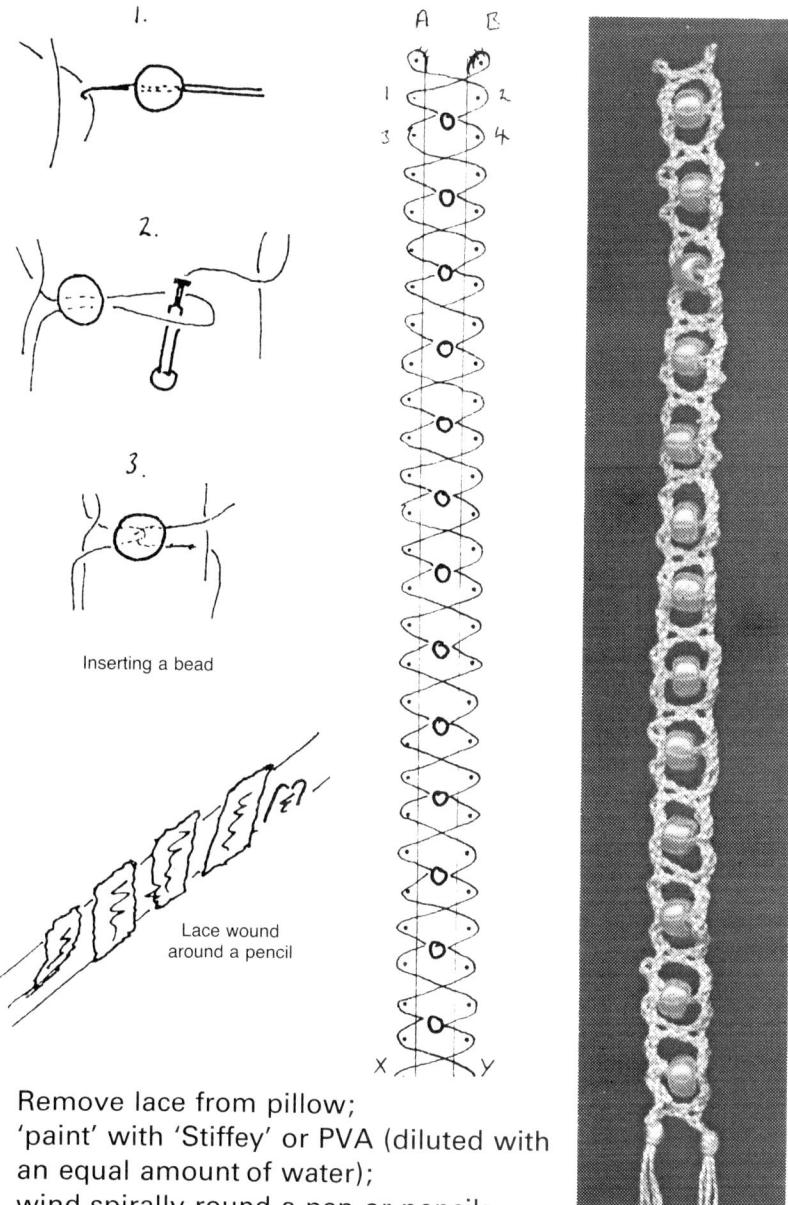

Inserting a bead

Lace wound around a pencil

Remove lace from pillow;
'paint' with 'Stiffey' or PVA (diluted with an equal amount of water);
wind spirally round a pen or pencil;
allow to dry.

Worked in white thread with clear or glittery beads this gives a quickly worked decoration for the Christmas tree.

J for juggernaut

Special Dentelles – 5prs for outline
6prs for wheels
12prs for filling

Start with 4prs across pin at A, taking the RH pr as wks work a wst braid along top and back of trailer, adding another passive pr at B and working turning stitches (see T for Teddy) as required.
For the wheel arches change to wst with dbls on the upper edge. Continue round the cab working the pointed front as for Unicorn ear.
Sew to start at A, sew and tie off at C.

Leave the LH pr for working filling and cut off remaining threads.
Sew in 2prs at each ringed pinhole (see V for Valentine),
1pr at A, and at each of the next 2 pins.
Tw every pr then work side of trailer in [½st.pin.½st] ground (see G for Goldfish) with spiders (see H for Horseshoe) or other features. Around the wheel arches

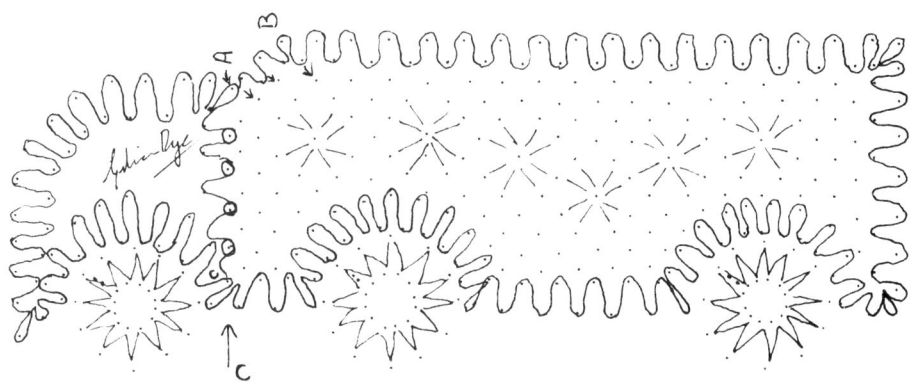

some of the pairs will need to be tied off and others sewn in later, while some are sewn in to go back into the work (also see V for Valentine). Finish at back of trailer by sewing in pairs and tying off with Bruges ties or reef knots (Q.3).

For the wheels hang 2prs on each of 3 pins across the tyre. Starting on L work:
* [2wst.tw wks.3wst.pin.tw wks];
  [3wst.tw wks.2wst.pin.tw wks].
Repeat from * all round, making sewings to wheel arches on either side. Finish with sewings to starting loops and a Bruges tie (see Q.3c).

Start of wheel

 for key

6 pairs Special Dentelles.

Start with 2prs on each of the arrowed pins, then work the main shaft using a different braid for each section as follows.

A-B wst.

B-C take second pair from edge as workers, 3 ½st, dbl, pin inside dbl (see bookmark section D).

C-D as for B-C but working wst instead of ½st and dbls.

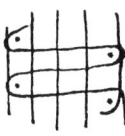

Working of C-D

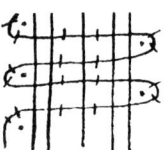

Working of D-E

D-E [2 wst.tw wks.wst.tw wks.2 wst].

E-F-G wst, discarding 2prs over the first 2 rows. At F [tw wks x2.sew in across the loop.tw wks x2] work 2 rows wst and repeat [ ].
Sew and Bruges tie (see Q.3c) to edge of braid at E.

Work remaining braids in wst with just 4prs, starting with 2prs on each of the pins at H, sewing off at I, then sewing in pairs to work J-K and L-M.

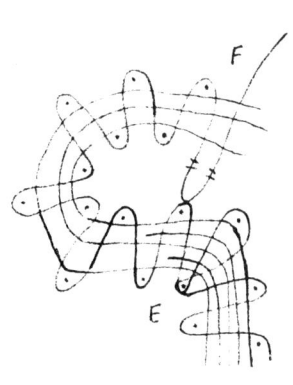

Working handle

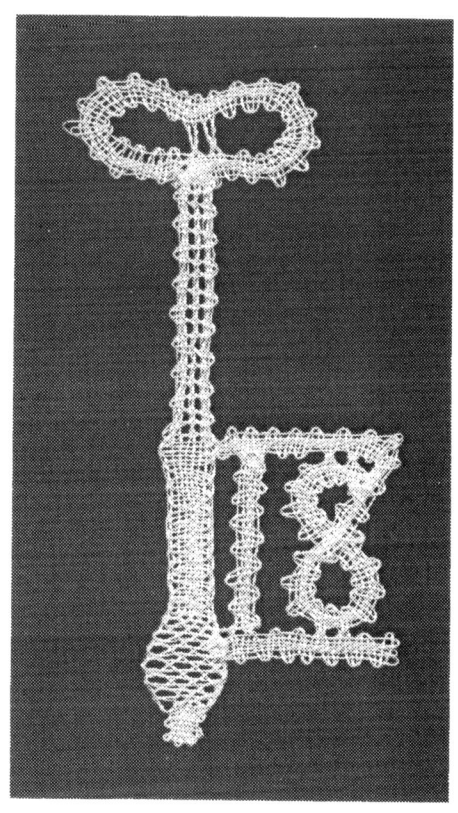

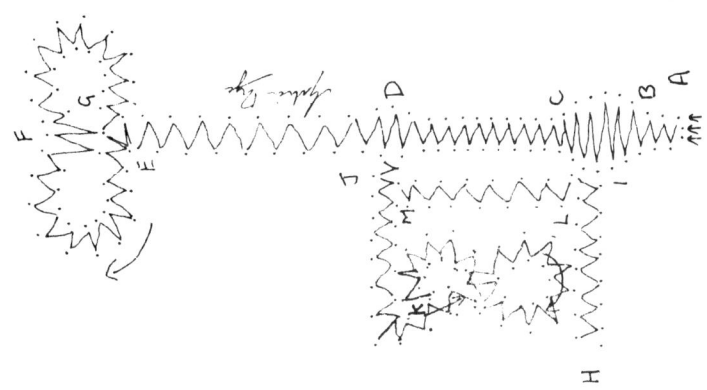

for lavender bag

9 pairs Sylko or Machine Broder 30.

Start with 2 prs on each of A & F
    1pr on each of B, C, D, E & G.
(The 2 prs on A, or the pair on G can be in a contrast colour if required).

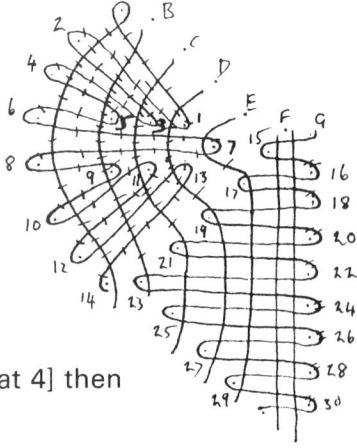

First work the Fan.
* Starting on the left work:
  [4 dbls. pin at 1]
Then working R to L: [4 dbls. pin at 2]
Next work [3 dbls. pin at 3] [3 dbls. pin at 4] then
[2 dbls. pin at 5] [2 dbls. pin at 6]
After pin 6 work [5 dbls. pin at 7]
              [5 dbls. pin at 8]
then [2 dbls.pin at 9] [2 dbls. pin at 10].
Continue second half to mirror first until pin 14 is in place.

Now work the triangle.
Take pair from G to work [2 wst.pin at 15]
[2 wst. tw wks x2. pin at 16]
[3 wst.pin at 17] etc. until [6 wst.pin at 23]
[6 wst. tw wks x2. pin at 24] at the widest point.
Next row is [5 wst.pin] etc.
After pin 30, leave the triangle and start second fan from *
remembering to twist pairs as they come from wst to dbls.

When three triangles and four fans have been completed work the corner section with:
2 rows of 5 dbls;
2 rows of 6 dbls, including one of the passives from the triangle; then 2 rows of 5 dbls.

Turn the pillow and repeat from *

Once the second side is started push down all the pins of the first fan and triangle, then you can start taking pins from the back of your work as you need them – leave most of the pins along each edge in place.

Finishing.
Work the extra part of the last corner then sew pairs to starting loops. Tie with reef knots (see Q.3b) and cut off.

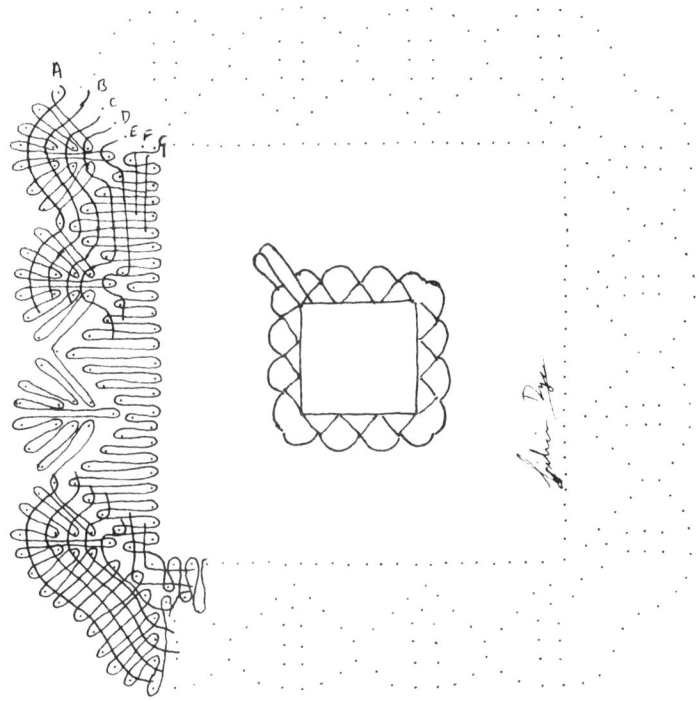

Make up a small bag just over 5cm square, fill with lavender (or stuffing for a pincushion).
Stitch lace in place taking stitches through loops left by pins.

Fold a length of narrow ribbon and stitch on either side of lace to cover join and make a hanging loop.

 *for mat*

6-9 pairs.
The sample was worked with 6prs in three different thicknesses of thread, producing a braid with a central cable. However the pattern could be worked entirely in Special Dentelles, without the cable, in which case 8 or 9 pairs would be needed.
Start with 5 pins across the braid at S, hang on:
   3prs Special Dentelles – 2prs on A, 1pr on E
   2prs Coton Perle 8 – 1pr on each of B and D
   1pr Coton Perle 5 – on C
With pairs from A work: dbl.pin at 1, then continue in basic braid with central cable:
*[tw wks.dbl.wst.cable (see Valentine).wst.tw wks.dbl.pin].
Repeat from *

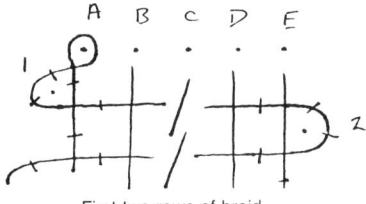

First two rows of braid   Sewing in a third loop

Twist workers more where there is a long loop around a pin – up to 10 twists on the very long loops.
Make sewings where pins are used twice. Where a pin is used 3 or 4 times only make a sewing on the last visit. Where the pricking is marked ᚐ work a dbl on the edge then pin beside the stitch, taking the pair that had been on the edge as wks for the next row. Sew and Bruges tie (see Q.3c) when threads return to S.

Work centre star with 2prs hung on T:
*[½st.tw RH pr x2.sew into two loops at U.tw x3.½st. pin at V].
Repeat from *
Bruges tie (see Q.3c) or darn ends into work.

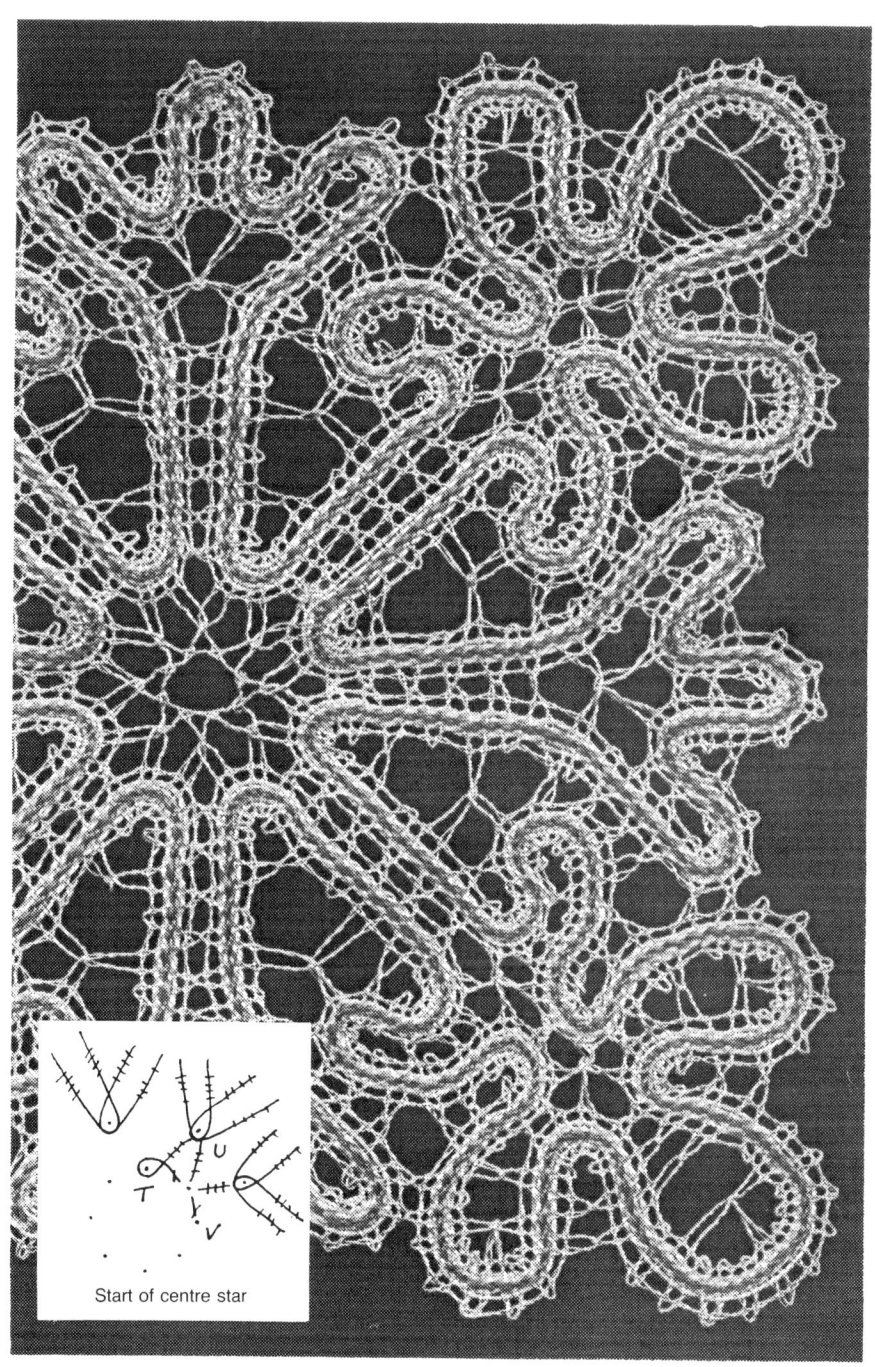

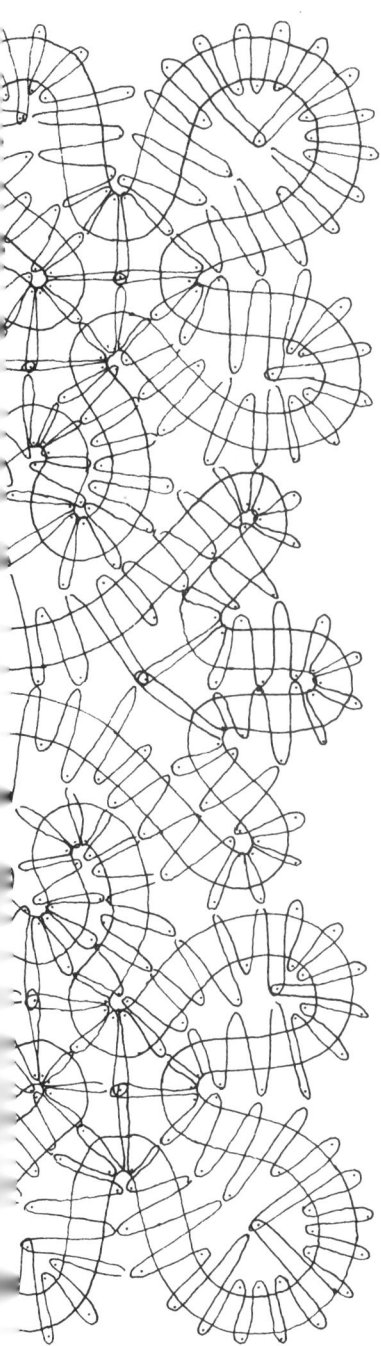

Working Diagrams for Necklace

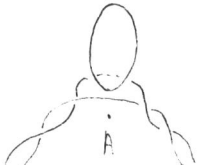

Passive pair with pendant
bead in position
(line = thread)

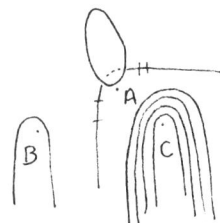

All pairs in position for start
(line = pair)

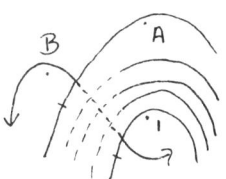

First row worked
(line = pair)

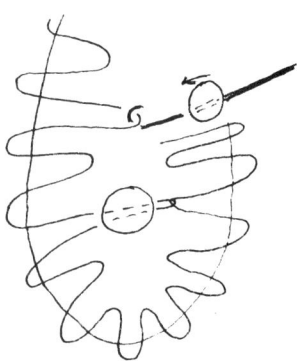

Adding bead to a loop

 *for necklace*

Materials:
   12prs Coton Perle 8 (2prs could be replaced with a contrast such as 'Goldfingering')
   16 beads (approx 5mm) with large centre hole
   1 pendant bead (optional)

Thread pendant bead on one pr before winding second bobbin, hang this and another pair across support pin A, tw x2 on each side.
Hang 2prs across B and remaining prs across C – if using contrasts they should be the lowest prs on C.
(The RH threads on A and C can be twisted temporarily round a pin to the side – see O for Octopus).
Take RH pr on B to work: [dbl (with LH pr from A)
   3 ½st.dbl (with LH prs from C).pin at 1].
Tw x2 LH pr on A and use this to start a ½st braid with dbls on each edge from pins 2-5 (put an extra tw on prs as they go round pins on the outside of curves).

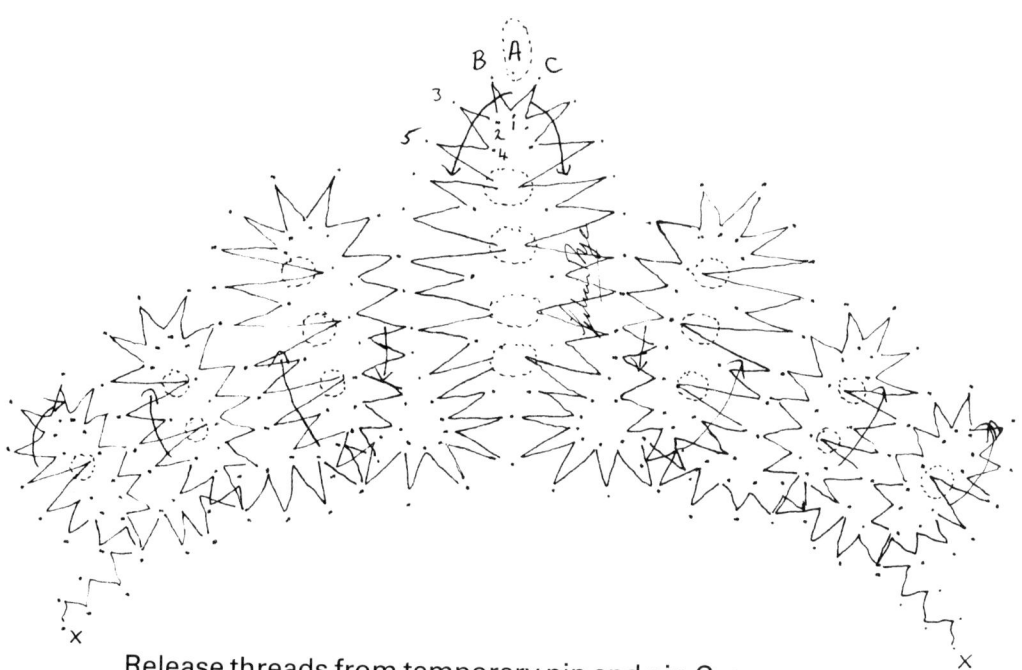

Release threads from temporary pin <u>and</u> pin C, ensure every pair is twisted. Take LH pr at 1 to work:
[dbl.3 ½st.dbl.tw wks.pin at C].
Work braid on this side to match that on L, bring both wk prs to centre and insert a bead (see I for Icicle).
Complete centre oval inserting a bead after each four rows on either side. Close at the top with ½st.pin.½st with the 2prs wks, then the 2 contrasts then wks again.
Leave the 6prs on the R and complete L side:
work round the outer curve of each oval in turn making a long twisted loop where a bead is wanted, then, as the curve closer to the centre is worked, slipping a bead on to the loop and making a sewing. Sewings should also be made wherever two braids touch and cross. Work ½st.pin½st where there is no room to work dbls on the inside of curves.
Reduce to 5prs after the 3-bead oval (by working 2prs together on the inside edge — see C for Candle).
After pin X work 1 row wst, discard 2 threads and work a 20-30 cm 4-strand plait with remaining threads (treating 2 bobbins as one). Cut threads and tie with an overhand knot (see Q.3a).
Work RH side to match L.

O for octopus

28 pairs Special Dentelles.

Start with 4prs across 1.
Twist the 4 threads on left around support pin A
(to reduce slipping while the RH side is worked).
Work a dbl with 2prs on R.
* Hang a new pair on support pin B.
Work ½st.pin (at 2). cr with this pair and
the 2prs from 1 (treating two threads as one);
dbl with 2prs on R, tw x2 pr on L.
Repeat from * until pin 12 is in place.

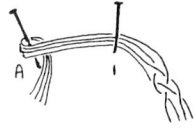
Starting with 4 pairs

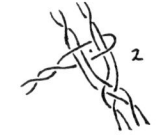
Bringing in a new pair

Release threads from A, work 2dbls with these.
Work L side (pins 13-23) to match R, hanging new pairs on support pin A.
Work body in ½st.pin.½st, inserting beads for eyes and following diagram for mouth.

Working mouth

Start working the arms once pin C is in position:
take RH pr on 12 to work * 3dbls.pin (at a).
Repeat from * until pin b is in place; tie one pair round the rest.
Trim ends.

Rewind 1pr, hang on pin x and work next arm as first.
Work 3rd arm with new pair hung on y.

The other arms are worked in a similar way.
2 prs hung on C as workers for the two centre arms, LH pair on 23 taken as wks for LH arm and other wks added as needed.

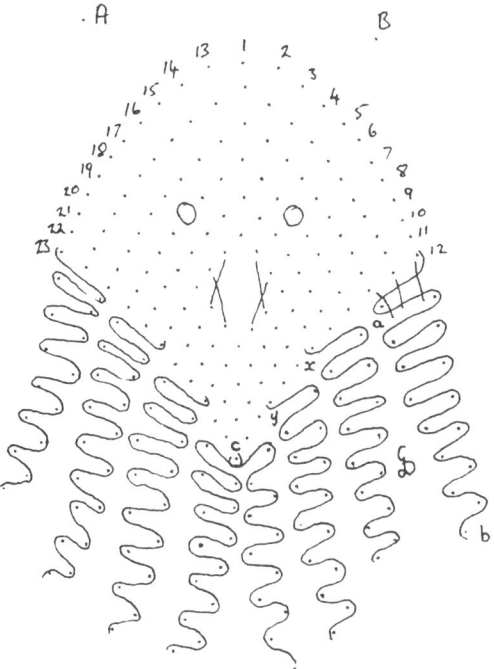
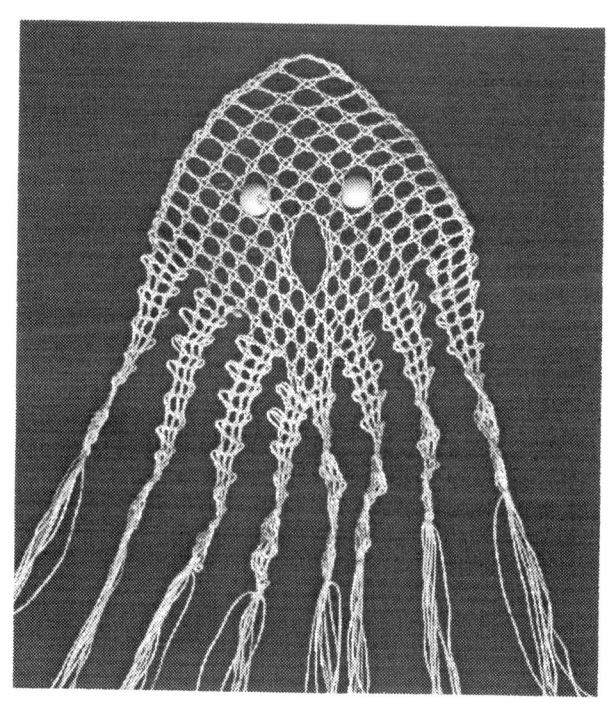

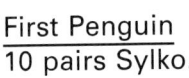 *for penguin*

Tip of wing

First Penguin
10 pairs Sylko.

Start with 4prs (passives) across pin A,
1pr wks on B.
Work wing and head in wst with dbls on the
outer edge, the first row will be:
[3 wst. tw wks. dbl. pin]
2nd row [dbl. 3 wst. tw wks x2].
Repeat these two rows.

Working of beak

Follow diagram for working inside of beak.
From D to E make sewings to edge of wing. As braid narrows discard 2 threads at a time from the wst (by turning to back of pillow to be cut close later).
Sew final 2 pairs to E, Bruges tie (see Q.3c), but do not cut close until the body has been worked.

For the body hang on pairs as indicated at the base, work 1 row in dbls then continue in ½st with dbls on free edges.
From F onwards make sewings to edge of the braid.
From E the work narrows so discard pairs as required after sewings – tie each discarded pair in a reef knot before cutting close. (It is only in whole stitch that threads can be discarded by just turning back then cutting close, threads discarded in ½st must be tied).

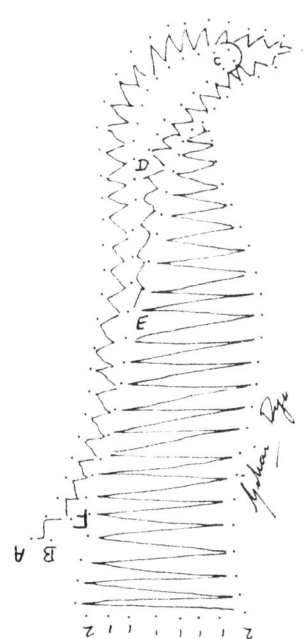 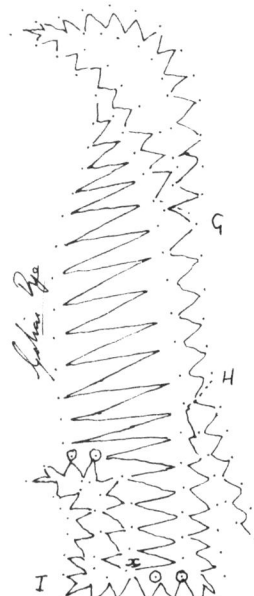

Penguin with Chick

Work wing and head as for first, then continue along back on top of braid already in place – use the same pins and make sewings at G and H.

Work round base, discard 1pr from wst at I, before working chick. Make 3 sewings to connect back and front of chick. Sew off to base braid, Bruges tie and cut off two pairs. Use the other 2prs, plus 2prs sewn in at each of the ringed pin-holes to work body in ½st with sewings to braids on either side and dbls on the edge above the chick.

Complete as for first penguin.

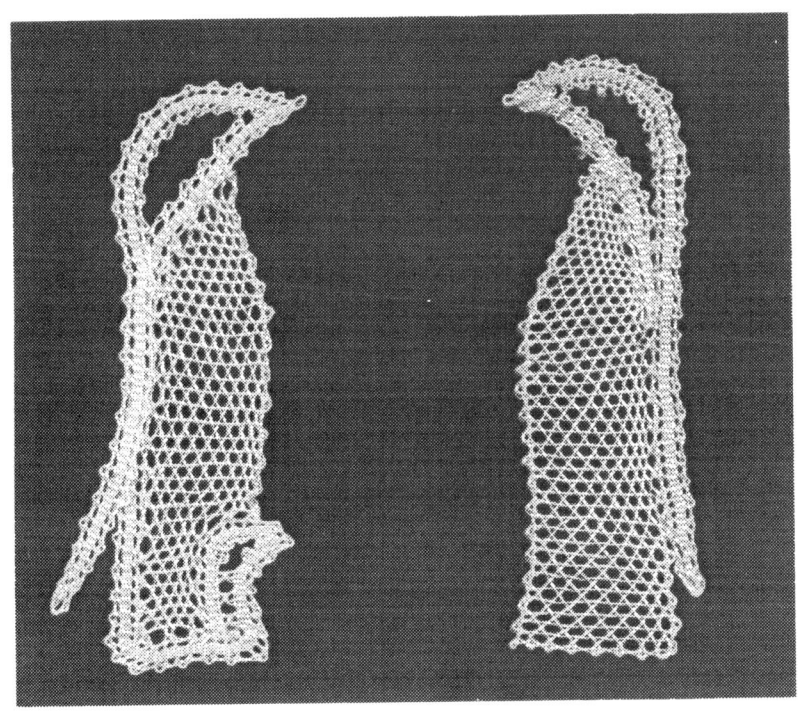

Q for queries

Q.1. What do I do if I am running out of thread on a bobbin?

– Before the end gets too short wind the bobbin with new thread, make a knot in the end and loop it over a pin, tuck the old end under the hitch on the bobbin and work with double thread for a short distance. Once the pins have been removed the loose ends can be trimmed close.

Starting a new thread

Threads worked double

Q.2. When do I take out the pins?

— For small items all the pins should be left in until the work is finished. With larger pieces pins may be removed once there is no chance of bobbins pulling against the stitches supported by those pins. Where the work is coming back on itself the pins should be pushed right down and covered by a cover cloth. Wherever possible all pins at the edge of the work should be left in position until at least a day after the work is complete — this allows the threads to 'set' in position. All tying of knots should be completed and bobbins cut off before final pins are removed.

Q.3. How do I finish off the ends?

— Different sorts of knot have been used in finishing the pieces in this book.

a) <u>Overhand knot</u> — for a tuft or fringe.
Cut two or more threads at least 8cm from the work.
Use a long pin to tie a simple knot in the threads, keep the pin in the knot while you ease it up to the work, only then pull the knot tight. Trim ends as required.

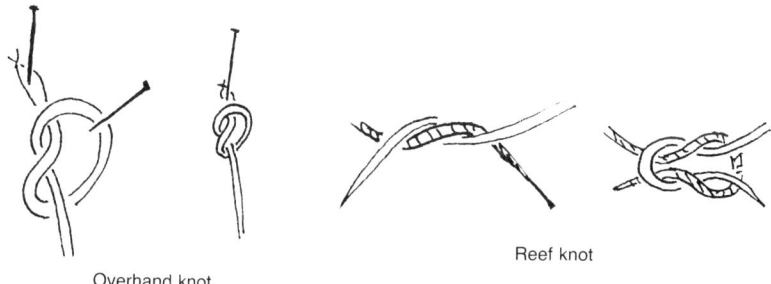

Overhand knot   Reef knot

b) <u>Reef knot</u> — for finishing individual pairs to be cut close.
Tie right over left, left over right, pull tight, without jerking, after each movement. This is done most easily with the bobbins still on the threads.
When work is complete cut threads as close as possible to the knot. With slippery or springy threads a <u>tiny</u> spot of PVA glue can be applied to the cut ends.

c) <u>Bruges tie</u> – for finishing 4 or more threads close together.
* Starting on L, tie first 2 threads R over L (as though starting a reef knot); throw bobbin now in R hand under L and pick up next bobbin along;
repeat from * to end of row; work back R to L, again tying R over L, but this time throwing L bobbin under R – pull all knots firmly without jerking.

1st knot of Bruges tie

2nd knot of Bruges tie

Q.4. What are tallies?

– Tallies are small woven blocks which can be square (or rectangular) leaf-shaped or triangular.

a) To work a <u>leaf-shaped tally</u>:
start with 2prs on one pin;
take 2nd bobbin from L as weaver;
hold other 3 bobbins between fingers of L hand;
weave single bobbin over and under;
keep outer threads taut as the shape widens, allow to come together as it narrows;
finish by tying the weaver once round the other threads.

Start of leaf-shaped tally

Finishing a leaf with a hitch

b) For a <u>square tally</u> start with 2prs on separate pins, tw x2:
take 2nd bobbin from L as weaver;
hold other 3 bobbins between fingers of L hand;
weave 4th bobbin over and under;
finish by twisting the weaver twice round the RH thread,
supporting each pair by a separate pin.

Square tally　　　　　　　　　　Triangular tallies

c) For a <u>triangular tally</u> start as a leaf and finish as a square, or vice versa.

Q.5. Can lace be stiffened?

– Yes. Use PVA or 'Stiffey' for a very stiff finish (see I for Icicle). For a less stiff finish spray lightly with hair spray or spray starch – leave work pinned in place, protect rest of pillow with paper before spraying. Caution: do not soak the lace or the pillow will be damaged, spray only from the distance recommended on the can, give two or three light sprays allowing to dry in between.

Q.6. What is the best way of mounting my lace?

– This depends on how it is to be used. If it is to go on a card for example then use <u>tiny</u> amounts of PVA, eg Marvin or Resin W (woodwork glue):
position the lace then * turn back one section and use a pin to apply tiny spots of PVA, press down and repeat from * until all areas are fixed.

If the lace is going on fabric then it should be stitched in place. Sometimes one or two stitches will be enough just to stop the lace moving when under glass, other pieces may need to be stitched all round – pin and tack in position first. Use a fine thread, the same colour as the lace and stitch into the holes where pins have been.

Mounting an edging

Mounting a motif on fabric

Q.7. Are there many different types of lace?

– Yes. Most of the lace in use today is machine made, but until the end of the 18th century all lace was made with needle or bobbins. There are many different styles of needle lace (known as needlepoints) and even more varieties of bobbin lace. The patterns in this book are for braid laces and simple torchon pieces. In the past England made commercially three other styles of bobbin lace – Honiton, Bucks point and Bedfordshire. Other European countries have their own traditional laces – Bruges, Cluny, Valenciennes etc. There are also lace-like fabrics made by other techniques such as crochet, tatting or knitting.

Q.8. When was lace invented?

— It is difficult to say exactly, but simple forms of both bobbin and needle lace were known before 1550. Techniques have developed and styles changed a great deal since that time.

Q.9. Where can I learn more about lacemaking?

— There are lacemaking groups and classes in most areas of the UK, some providing tuition for children as well as adults — your local library may have details. The national (and international) organisation for lacemakers is The Lace Guild. If you contact the Guild headquarters at 'The Hollies', 53 Audnam, Stourbridge, West Midlands, DY8 4AE, they can put you in touch with other lacemakers in your area. Membership of the Lace Guild is open to all who are interested in lace. The Guild arranges courses and exhibitions and provides many services for lacemakers, including an extensive library and a growing collection of lace and other items for study.

Members receive a quarterly magazine with articles, patterns and details of lace days, exhibitions, suppliers etc. There is a separate Young Lacemakers Club with its own newsletter.

Q.10. Are there any qualifications in lacemaking?

— Lacemaking can be taken as part of GCSE or A-Level Textiles, as one of the skills for the Duke of Edinburgh award, and as a City and Guilds Creative Studies qualification. Also The Lace Guild provides independent assessment for adults and children at beginner, intermediate and advanced levels.

 *for rabbit*

7 pairs Sylko.

This motif has been worked in a variety of stitches — ½st with dbls on each edge for ears, wst for head, dbls for body, ½st with dbls on outer edge only for tail — other combinations could be used.
Start at A with 4prs laid across the pin, work as for Candle flame, adding pairs at the next 3 pins.
Turning stitches will be needed at B, C, G & H.
Change to wst at B and discard one pair (by turning two bobbins to the back of the pillow).
For the whiskers tw wks 4 or 5 times going out to the pin and 4 or 5 times back.
Discard another pair on the row before C then change to dbls.
At D change to ½st with dbls on outer edge and at E sew off to edge of braid and Bruges tie (see Q.3c).

Start second side with 4prs on F and work to match first, making sewings where the two sides touch.

For a turning stitch the wks work a wst or dbl with the inside pair which then becomes the wks for the next row.

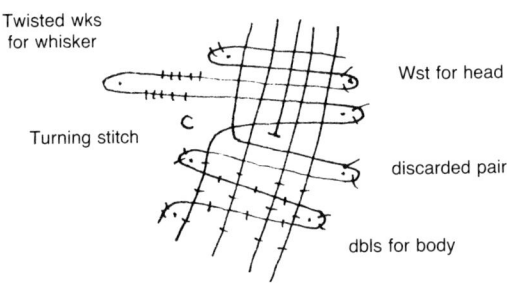

Stitches at change from head to body

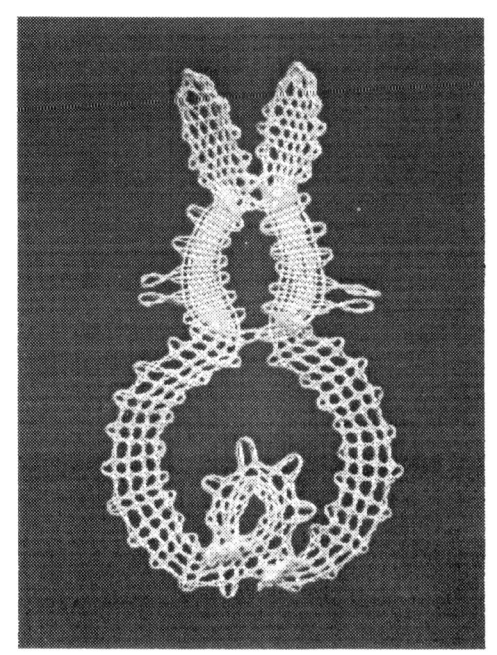

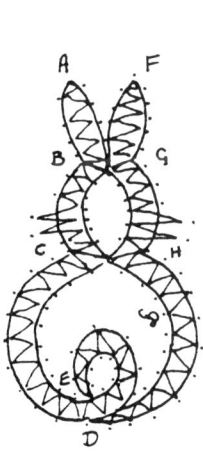

Pattern for working in Sylko

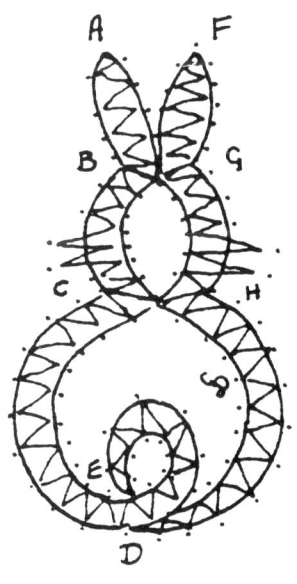

Pattern for thicker thread

# S for seahorse

10 pairs Special Dentelles.

Start with 2prs across each of pins A, B & C.
Work 1 row dbls R to L, put in pin 1 to the R of the last stitch.
Take RH of these prs to work:
[3 ½st.dbl.pin at 2]. Add a new pr on 2 (see C for Candle), next row: [dbl. 4 ½st. dbl. pin beside stitch].
Continue head in ½st with dbl.pin.dbl on R, dbl.pin beside stitch on L.
Add new pairs on pins marked ▼
After pin D work [dbl.4 ½st.pin at E.½st]. The braid splits here with both pairs on E becoming wks: take each to the outside and back to centre then insert a bead (see I for Icicle).

Change to dbls for the RH braid, keeping ½st on L – on the tight inside curve work just a ½st putting pin beside the stitch. Where the two braids meet work ½st.pin.½st.

After putting in pin F hang on 2prs and work through in wst, use these prs to work a plait (tw.cr repeated as often as necessary), going out to the points and back. Where the plait touches the braid treat the two prs as one to work wst.pin.wst with the wks.

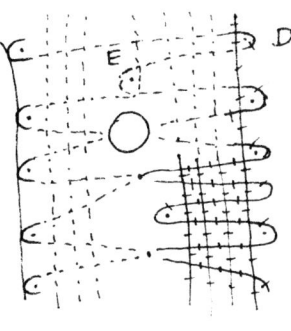

Dividing the braid and working the eye

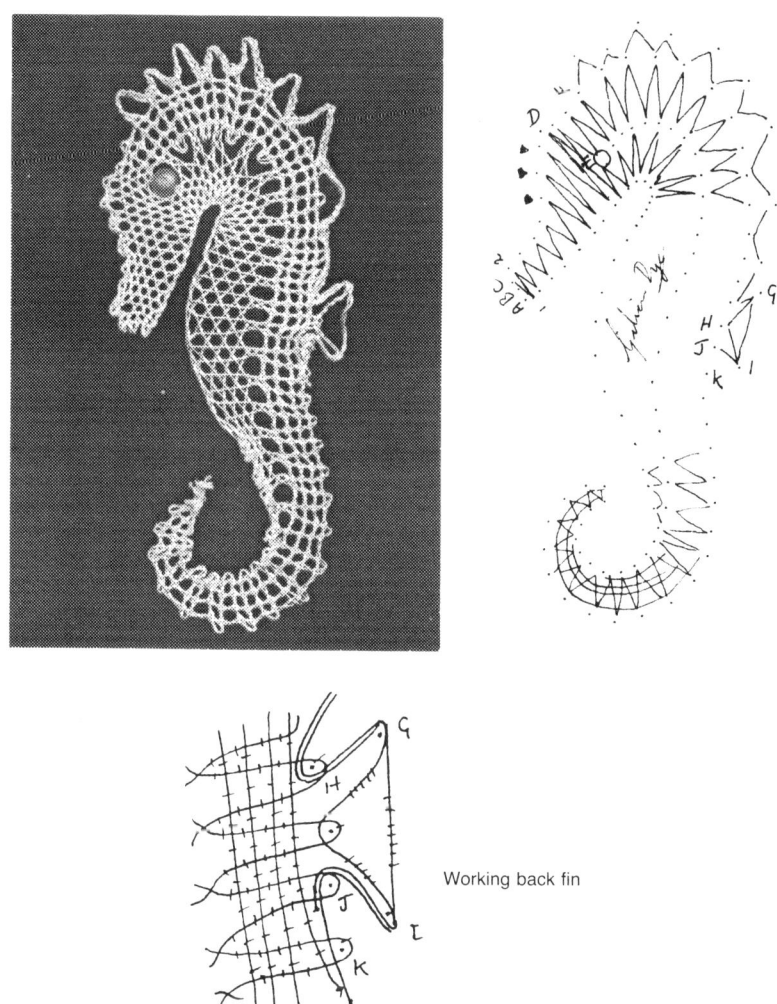

Working back fin

At G tw RH pr x7; LH pr tw x5. wst (with wks).pin at H.wst.tw x5. wst with pr left on G.pin at I, plait to J.

Dbl.pin.dbl at J treating each of the pairs of the plait as one thread then discard one of each pair.
At K work together the edge pair and the remaining prs from the plait, discard two threads.
Similarly on LH edge, as the work narrows, work two prs together and discard two threads. (See Y for Yacht). Bruges tie (see Q.3c) final 3prs at tip of tail.

T for teddy bear

4 pairs Sylko.

Start with 3prs (passives) side by side on pin S, 1pr (workers) on A.
Work along chin and around head in wst. From B to C and D to E work [2 wst. tw wks. dbl] going from inside to out, and [dbl. 2 wst] from outside in.

Working of ear   Turning stitch

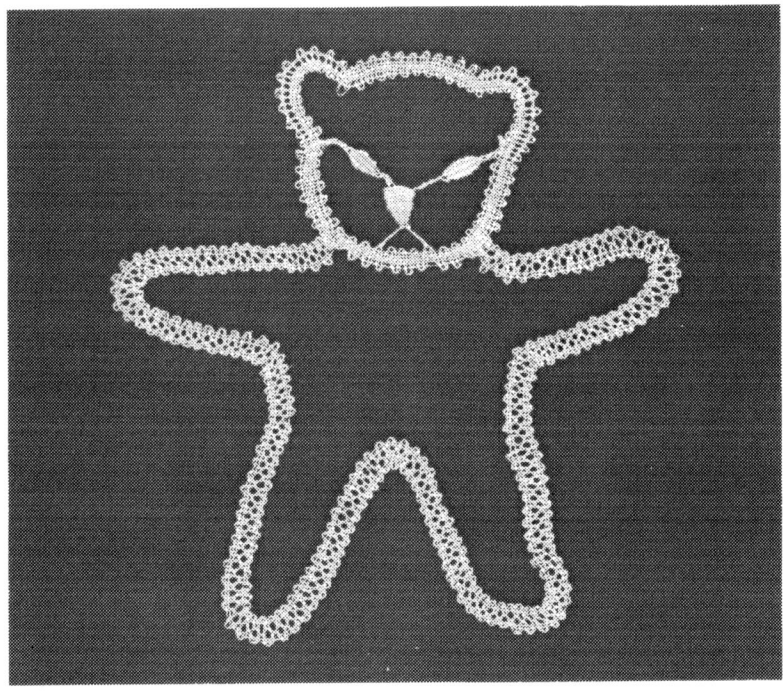

At C and other places where there is no pin, work a turning stitch, ie work to the edge, leave the workers to become passives and take the last pair of passives worked as the new workers.

When S is reached make sewings (see A for Alphabet) to 2 of the starting loops, then work around arms and legs. In the sample the braid used for this is:

[wst. tw wks. ½st. wst. pin].

On reaching F make sewings to the edge of the braid. Tie threads with a Bruges tie (see Q.3c) and cut close.

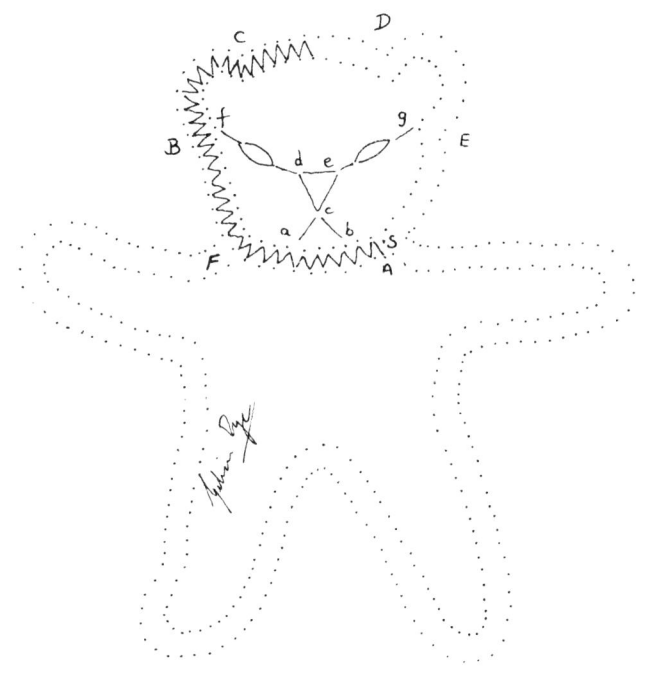

For face sew in a pair at each of a and b, twist each pair 3 times and make a triangular tally from c to d-e. At each of pins d & e add another pair and work a short plait, then a leaf-shaped tally and another plait for each eye. Sew in and tie off at f and g.

Spray lightly with hair spray and leave to 'set' before removing from pillow.

 *for unicorn*

This is worked entirely in wst using 4prs Special Dentelles – the centre passives can be replaced by a fine silver or glittery-white thread.

Work the head and body in 3 sections:
A-B, C-D and E-F, making sewings at shared pin-holes – where the braids are close together do not twist before or after the sewing.

Working of ear

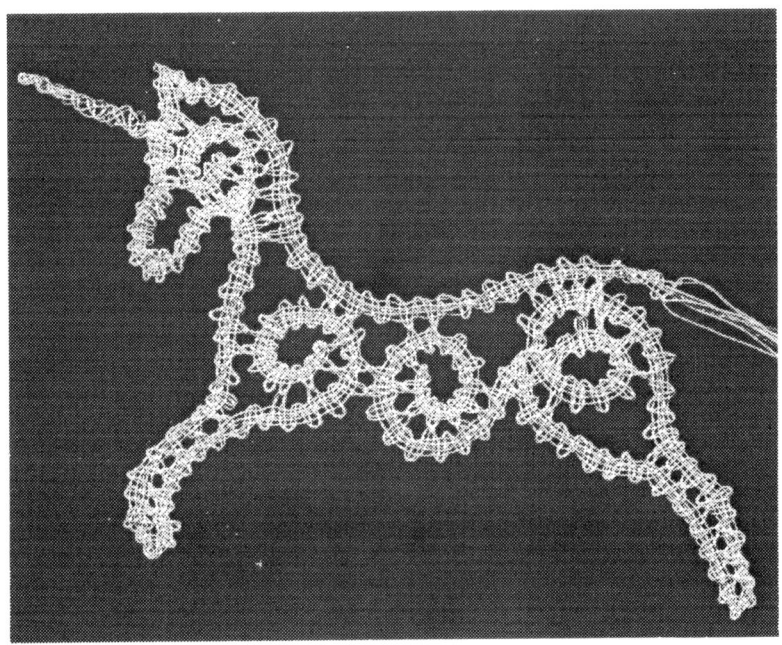

Follow diagram for working of ear – the turn at x is worked in the same way.

At B tie the two RH threads and the two LH, then cut all threads to give a tail.

At D & F (and H) sew to edge of braid and Bruges tie (see Q.3c).

Work horn from G-H, also in wst, but always working from L to R – see diagram.

Working of horn

V for valentine

These can be worked as simple outlines, or with fillings. The sample shown has an outline worked in wst with a central cable and a filling of torchon ground with some of the stitches replaced by beads. There are many other possibilities using different braids or fillings within the ground.

Outline: 5prs Special Dentelles
         + 1pr Coton Perle 8 (for cable).
Start with 1pr (workers) on a and remaining pairs, side by side on b with the thicker threads in the centre. Work all round with:
  [2 wst. cable. 2 wst. tw wks x2. pin] on each row.

1st row

For the cable: lift RH bobbin of contrast pair, pass both wks under this thread and over the other thread of the pair, put the raised bobbin down to the left of its partner.

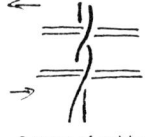
2 rows of cable

Work turning stitches on the inside of the point, ie work to the edge, leave the workers to become passives and take the last pair of passives worked as the new workers.

When the outline is complete 'sew' (see A for Alphabet) pairs to starting loops and tie off with a Bruges tie (see Q.3c) omitting cable pair.
If working a filling leave the two pairs closest to a and cut off remainder.

For the filling: sew in 1 or 2 pairs at each of the ringed pin holes, twist each pair and work in torchon ground – ½st. pin. ½st,

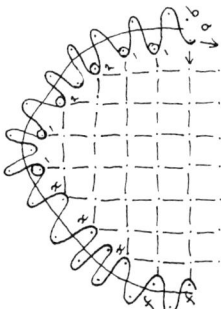

sewing pairs into the edge of the braid and taking them back into the ground as required (eg at x in diagram).

Where pairs are no longer required sew and tie off (f).

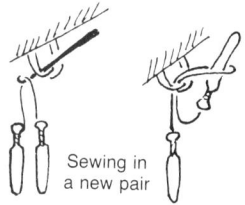
Sewing in a new pair

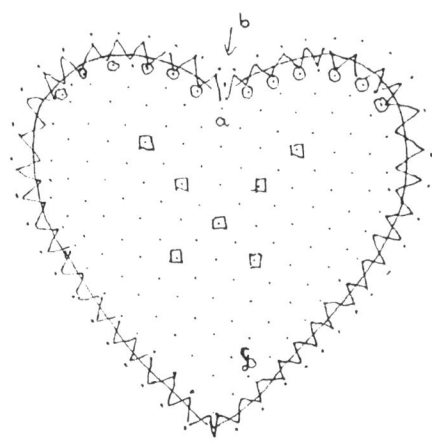

The squares on the pattern show where beads have been inserted for the sample (see I for Icicle) in place of a stitch.

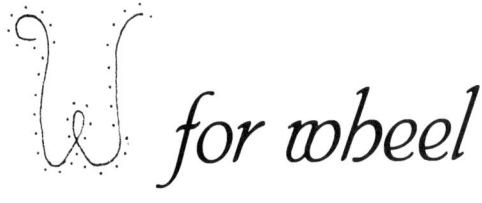 *for wheel*

7 pairs Coton Perle 8.

Start with 1pr passives hung on each of A to F.
1pr wks on G.
*Work a row of dbls from R to L, pin, then dbls from L to R, pin.

Now put extra twists in the passives as indicated on the pricking, ie the inside pair keeps one twist, the next is given an extra twist to make 2, 2 extra twists on the next and so on.
Repeat from *

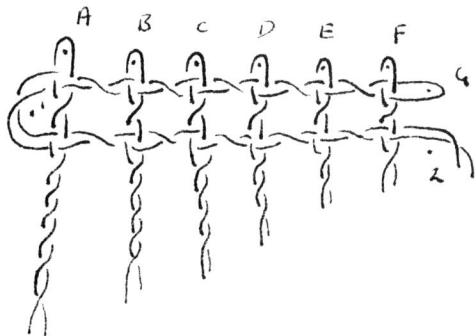

When the wheel is complete sew each pair to its starting loop and tie in a firm reef knot (see Q.3b).
The threads from A could be kept for a hanging loop while the remainder are cut close.

By using different combinations of thickness and colour of thread many variations are possible with this simple pattern. Try a thick glitter yarn (eg 'Goldfingering') as workers with toning or contrasting threads for passives.

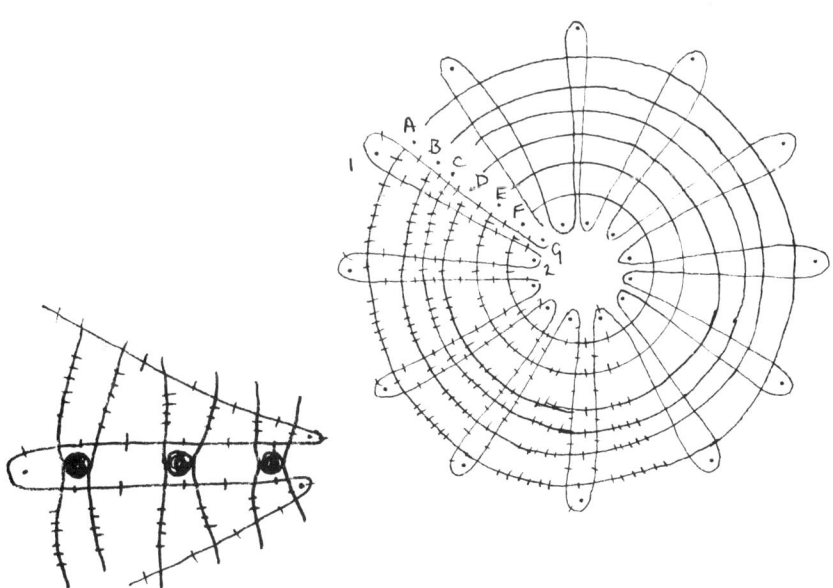

It is also possible to insert beads between passives within the spokes (see I for Icicle).

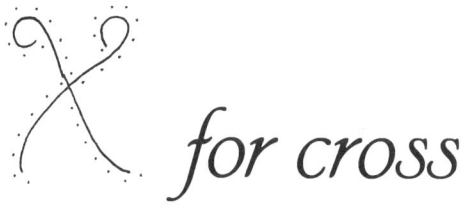 *for cross*

9 pairs Sylko – 7prs main colour, 2prs contrast.

This is worked as an edging (starting at the foot and working all round) using the same triangles and fans as the Lavender Bag.

Start with 2prs at A and work first triangle bringing in a pair at each arrowed pin-hole.
Where wks go to midline pin-holes (m) twist x5 – when the second half is worked: [tw wks x2. sew. tw x2].
Hang the 2 contrast pairs on B for start of first fan.
For the central pin of the cross (C) take the second pair of passives through wks and other passives, tw x9 around pin and back through 2prs – this will be done 3 times and on the 4th turn wks should be twisted x4, sewn into all 3 loops, tw x4.

Follow the pricking for the extended fans on the outer turns – the longest row of dbls includes all the passive pairs.

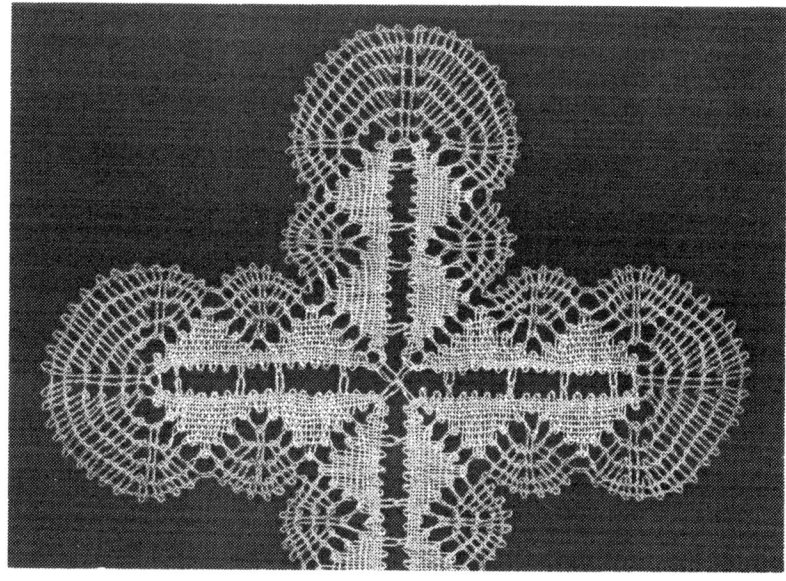

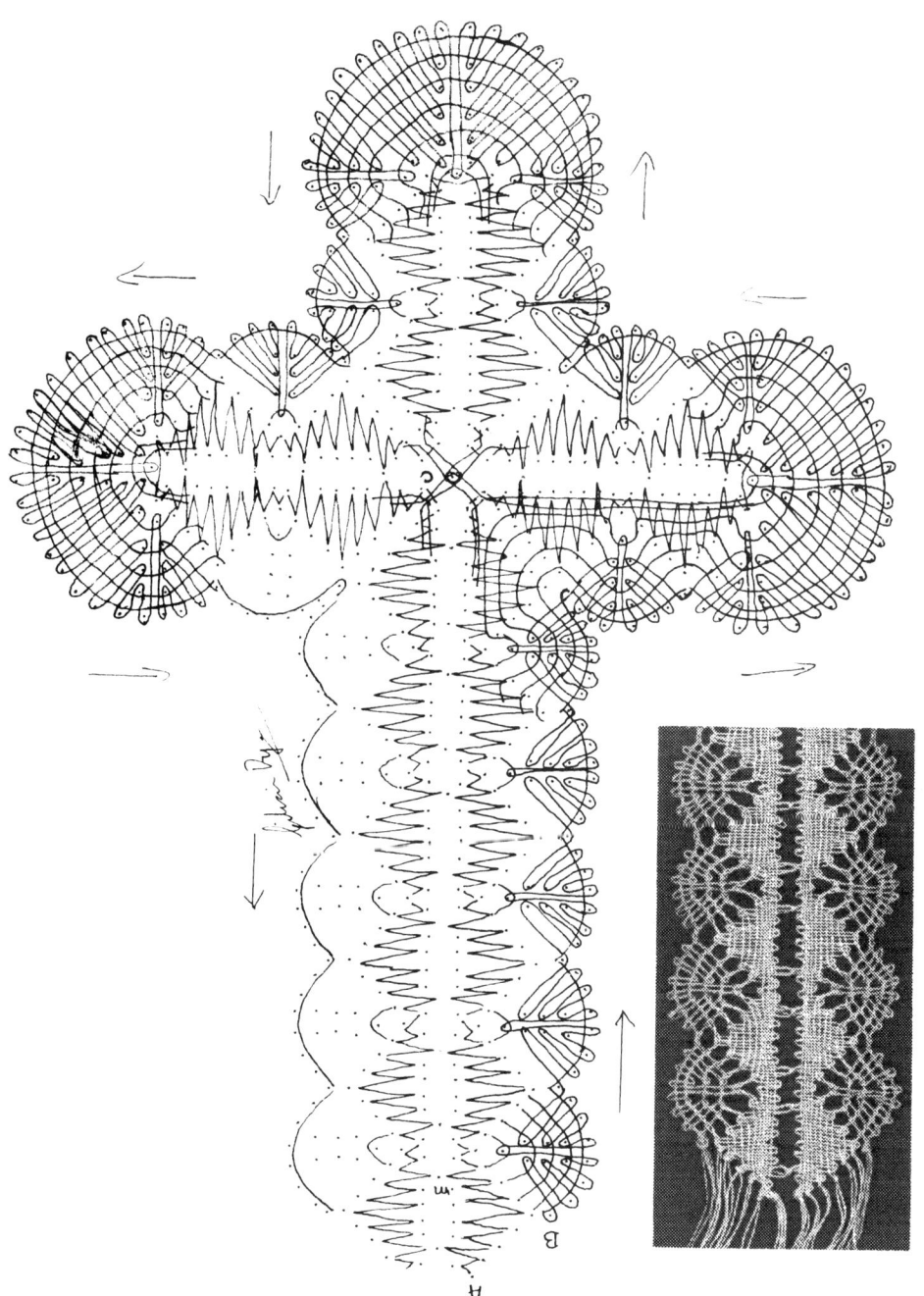

Finish with overhand knots (see Q.3a).
Cut short lengths of thread and sew into starting loops to match finish.

 *for yacht*

Worked in Sylko.

Work the <u>hull</u> first, in wst starting with 2prs on A and adding a pair at each of the pins on the R until 10prs are in use. After B start reducing the number of prs by turning back 3rd and 5th passives from R on alternate rows until 3prs are left at point. Work a plait with these, turn the plait back and tie down with 2 of the discarded pairs.

Next work the <u>mast</u> in wst with 3prs, started on C and sewn and tied off to the hull at D.

Each of the <u>sails</u> is worked in ½st with dbls on outside edge. For the smaller sail start with 2prs on E and add a pr at each of the outer pins until 12prs are in use, making sewings to the mast where pins are shared.

For the bottom of the sail either:
work a row of dbls from F to G, sew wks to mast and tie each of the other prs in an overhand knot;
or: dbl.pin.dbl at F; treat these 2prs as 1pr to * work dbl.pin.dbl with next pr from sail; discard 1 thread from each of the double ones; treat the remaining 2prs as one and repeat from *; sew and tie off final 2 or 3prs at G.

Working bottom of sail

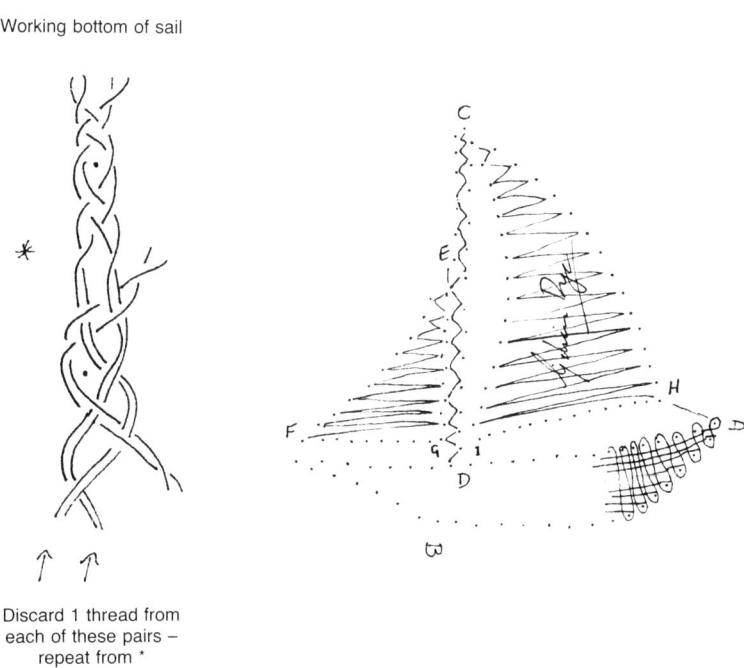

Discard 1 thread from each of these pairs – repeat from *

The larger sail is worked in a similar way, started with 2prs sewn in at the pin below C and pairs added until 15 are in use (the inner edge is only sewn to the mast at I). Before finishing the bottom edge, from H to I, 1pr from H can be twisted and sewn and tied off at A.

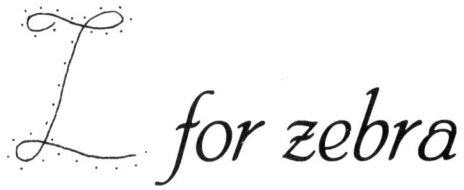
for zebra

20-30 pairs white Coton Perle 8 (10prs tied off for the mane can be brought into use again).
Plus 1 pair gimp of thick black wool or Coton Perle 5 wound double.

(For a horse motif the pattern could be worked without the gimp).

Start with 3prs on A: hang 2prs across the pin; hang on 3rd pr taking 1 bobbin over the 2 threads on the right, the other under them.

Bring in a pair at each arrowed pin hole with ½st.pin.½st (hang in turn on a support pin).

Hang 2prs on pin B, work ½st.tw with these before working ½st.pin.½st at C and ½st.pin.dbl at D.

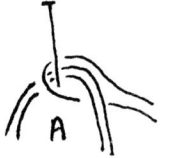

Starting 3prs at A

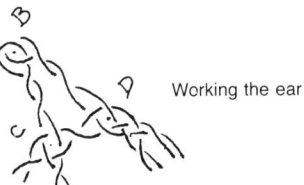

Working the ear

Twist twice on each side of gimp

Work ½st.pin.½st at E and F, then bring in the gimp before working G.
Work in ½st.pin.½st, taking the gimp on either side of pins G to H, then working the two together towards D, discard 1 gimp (to be cut close later).
Work a square tally (see Q.4b) or insert a bead (see Icicle) for the eye.
Continue in ½st.pin.½st;
taking gimp along solid line, finishing off pairs for the mane as follows: treat the 2prs from D as 1pr to work ½st.pin.cr; work a dbl with the double pair; tie the single pair in an overhand knot (see Q.3a).

Add 1pr at I, hanging on the new pair as for A before working the ½st after the pin.

Add 2prs at each pin marked ⇒ hanging across a support pin then using existing edge pair to work:
dbl with RH pr.pin. dbl with LH pr, release from support pin.

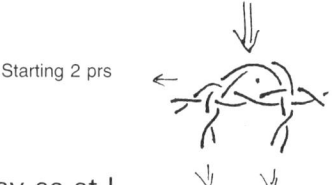

Starting 2 prs

Add 1pr at J in the same way as at I.
Turn pillow and complete front leg, working dbl.pin.dbl on each edge while continuing with ½st.pin.½st for inner pins.

At each of the bottom pins tie 2prs with an overhand knot and cut close.

Return to original direction of work and complete back.

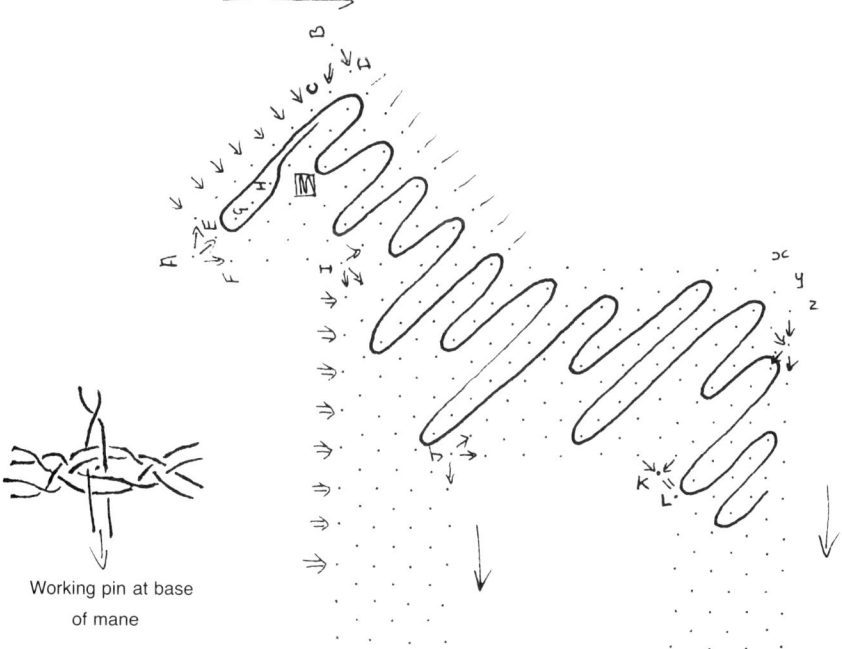

Working pin at base of mane

When work reaches z turn pillow and work hind leg as for front.
At L treat the 2prs from K as 1pr to work dbl.pin.dbl, then discard 2 threads.

Plait pairs from x, y and z to form tail, tie one thread round rest, trim.
Trim mane.

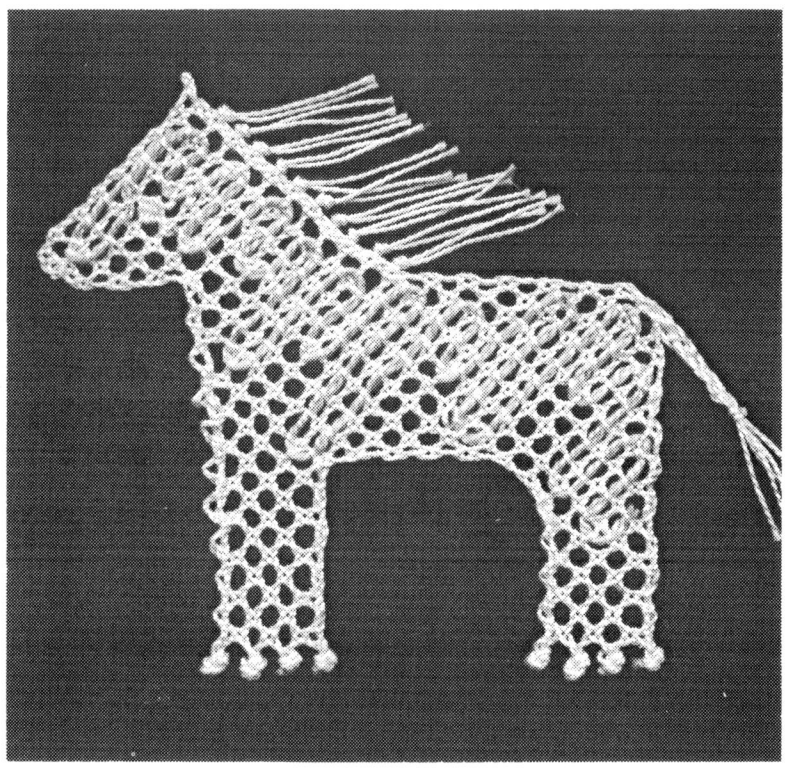